A Case for Shylock

Gareth Armstrong was born in Wales and graduated in Drama from Hull University. He has worked extensively as an actor and director in regional theatre, and appeared in the West End and the Royal Shakespeare Company.

When an Associate Artist at Salisbury Playhouse he wrote his solo play, *Shylock*, which he has since performed over six hundred times in more than thirty countries. The show continues to tour worldwide for the British Council and regularly plays throughout North America.

Shylock has been translated and performed in Catalan, Spanish and Italian, with productions planned in French, Dutch, Romanian and Hebrew.

Gareth Armstrong also records audio-books, commentaries and voice-overs, and is a frequent broadcaster with the BBC. He was a member of *The Archers* cast for many years.

by the same author

SHYLOCK

published by
The Players' Account
ISBN 0 95366 470 8

A Case for Shylock

Around the World with Shakespeare's Jew

GARETH ARMSTRONG

Foreword by Judi Dench

NICK HERN BOOKS
London
www.nickhernbooks.co.uk

A Nick Hern Book

A Case for Shylock
first published in Great Britain in 2004
by Nick Hern Books Limited
14 Larden Road, London w3 7st

Copyright © 2004 Gareth Armstrong

Foreword copyright © 2004 Judi Dench

Gareth Armstrong has asserted his moral right
to be identified as the author of this work

Typeset by Country Setting
Kingsdown, Kent, ct14 8es

Printed and bound in Great Britain
by Biddles, King's Lynn

A CIP catalogue record for this book
is available from the British Library

isbn 1 85459 785 x (hardback)
isbn 1 85459 822 8 (paperback)

To Frank Middlemass
and Geoffrey Toone

'Old friends are best'

Contents

Foreword ix
by Judi Dench

PART ONE
Out of the Ghetto 5
R.I.P 8
From Ambridge to Africa 11
A Rustic Revolution 25
Roots and Branching Out 28
Steve 33
Last-Chance Saloon 39
Finding the Plot 42
Playing with Paranoia 51

PART TWO
The Shock of the Old 63
Enter Tubal 69
Posing as an Israelite 74
Flying Solo 86
Swans and Kiwis 94
Macbeth and Mickey Mouse 99
Getting in a State 105
Two Exits to Thunderous Silence 114

PART THREE

Swastikas and Sadomasochism 127
The Case for Shylock 137
Lost in Translation 147
Bloodsuckers 152
State of the Union 162
Beyond Belief 168
Shylock Wallah 178
Bloody Justice 194
Some of the People, Some of the Time 198
Back to the Ghetto 203

Acknowledgements 207

Foreword

Reading Gareth Armstrong's book reminded me of why I like and admire actors so much. He has the actor's gift of being totally serious about his work without taking himself seriously.

To be an actor is to remain a child. By this I do not mean childishness, but a child-like ability to remain playful and, just as importantly, constantly inquisitive. Reading this delightfully funny and moving book, one is constantly reminded of this. Incidents are related with a genuine humility, the wide-eyed, curious child looking at the world through the worldly, critical eyes of the adult. What could so easily have been an ego-trip round the world is turned into a rich, warm and moving portrait of humanity, with all its flaws, follies, generosity, greed, hatred and warmth. The reactions to his show are fantastically diverse and occasionally frightening, but this is theatre, and in the controversial outcast figure of Shylock he could not have picked a better subject to reflect in Hamlet's mirror the many faces of a curious world.

The memories of West Africa, which I visited on two occasions, came flooding back. Reading of Valerie West, who was with the British Council and was instrumental in organising the Nottingham Playhouse tour to West Africa, reminded me of a journey from Kano to Kaduna when James Cairncross suggested the first line of a limerick: 'One Christmas Miss Valerie West . . . ' After hours on a dusty road, I came up with:

One Christmas Miss Valerie West
Laid the Nottingham Playhouse to rest:
   O'er the thirty sad graves
   Of these thespian braves
Cried, 'I *was* only doing my best.'

One of the most endearing and enduring aspects of theatre is its ability to be deadly serious whilst being completely ephemeral and ever so slightly frivolous. Anyone who reads this book will get some inkling of one of the reasons we act: the insatiable desire to discover something, anything, about ourselves that we cannot find out any other way.

JUDI DENCH

A CASE FOR SHYLOCK

PART ONE

Out of the Ghetto

I woke that morning to row upon row of eyeless faces: some deathly white, some livid, all grotesque. With huge noses below their empty sockets they stared unseeingly at the ceiling or unnervingly straight above my head, lifeless and sinister. The walls of the apartment were lined with shelf upon shelf of what looked like death masks waiting to be brought back to life. Guerrino took his work home with him.

So often in Italy you see faces that look as if they have just stepped out of an Old Master: a wrinkled lady at a market straight from Caravaggio, or a workman who could be a double for a Veronese disciple. Guerrino is definitely a Michelangelo. He could be a younger, neater-bearded version of God from the ceiling of the Sistine Chapel, with a magnificent head and piercing eyes.

As the creative hub of one of the finest mask-makers in Venice, Guerrino's tiny shop is bursting at the seams, and he is in constant demand for movies, extravaganzas and even to work on the endless restoration of the Fenice Theatre. On the day we met he was happy to accept a commission from me for a Pantalone mask but warned me that I might have to wait a year, or maybe two.

He fed us black, chewy coffee and almond biscuits before Luca and I set off to trudge the city, neither of us keen to join the queues of serious sightseers. By midday we thought we had earned a drink and were happily sipping our first Bellinis, when Luca's mobile phone rang. Several elegant heads turned towards us in disapproval.

'Si ... si ... si ... si ... ' A long pause. 'Si.'

I am sure he said something else besides, but that is more or less the extent of my Italian. He rang off.

'Sheeet!' he said. 'This was Eugenio's agent. He says he is broke his knee and is in the 'ospital. He can no do the premiere tomorrow.'

The whole excuse for being in Venice, sitting in Florian's in St Mark's Square, drinking secco and apricot cocktails that cost almost as much as the flight to Italy, was to see Eugenio do the premiere. Luca had spent nearly three years battling the mind-boggling bureaucracy that be-devils everything in his country to try and mount my play in Venice. He had coped with delays and postponements, fiscal fiascos and artistic tantrums. And now, the day before our first night, we were facing cancellation.

Luca swiftly drained his glass and sped off to a crisis meeting at the theatre. For the rest of the day I mooched disconsolately along the canals, for once impervious to the city's magic.

In the late afternoon I went home to the Ghetto.

Guerrino's flat is on the top floor. He let down a stepladder and took me onto his tiny roof garden to watch the sunset. Because the Ghetto became too small for its original inhabitants, who were forbidden to live anywhere else, they extended their houses in the only way they could. Up. In my melancholy state it was all the more affecting to look out across the rooftops of Venice in the fading light to the vastness of St Mark's Square and the lagoon beyond. Can there be anywhere else with so fine a view of the city? Apart from the television aerials, it might be the vista that Shylock saw. If he ever ventured onto his roof.

When Luca got back from his meeting, he wouldn't tell me how it had gone until after we had eaten. Italians are like that. First he assured me that there was no way Eugenio was going to do the performance with an injured knee. Italians are like that too. There was a solution though. Would I be prepared to perform the show myself?

'Without my costumes, my props . . . my trunk?'

'Si.'

'Without my music, my lighting effects?'

'Si.'

'For a Venetian audience . . . in English?'

'Yes!'

When I arrived at the theatre next morning, there were six very beautiful young women with clipboards and sharpened pencils waiting to do my bidding. One was despatched to find a battered cabin trunk, another a black coat, hat and waistcoat, another to track down two wigs (one black, one ginger). A commedia false nose. A walking stick. A lawyer's neck tabs. A copy of *The Merchant of Venice*. A Gideon Bible. A box of Imodium.

I had reason to be nervous. Shylock was coming home.

R.I.P.

I love obituaries. The ones in the *Daily Telegraph* are best. Other people must think so too because they get published in collections with subtitles like 'Military' or 'Eccentric'.

The military dead, all officers, of course, have wonderful names. Usually double-barrelled, there's almost always a nickname too, squeezed within quote marks: Lt. Colonel 'Stumpy' Tossington-Boothe MC, etc . . . Maddeningly, they rarely explain why 'Stumpy', so you have to use your imagination. I speed-read the columns on his distinguished war service, and the commendations for bravery, to get to the really uneventful bits: 'After leaving the army, Tossing-ton-Boothe devoted himself to country pursuits in his be-loved Loamshire. His chairmanship of the Royal Society for Distressed Stable Boys brought him great satisfaction . . . '

Fifty years of dogs and guns and wellies and grooms in reduced circumstances. After a decade of bravery and adventure, it reads like half a century of anti-climax. Is that how Stumpy felt or was he just glad to have survived it all? And beyond the mentions in despatches, what was the real Stumpy like? A good obit writer gives lots of scope for reading between the lines, like the subtext in a good play: 'In Egypt, "Stumpy" was a legend in the officers' mess', meaning he was a noisy piss-artist. Or 'Tossington-Boothe was never one to suffer fools gladly', meaning he was a right bastard.

Roy Kinnear was a wonderful English character actor, who died after falling from a horse while making a movie. Stumpy would have thought that a great way to go, but

Kinnear was nowhere near ripe enough for the reaper. He was much loved and much missed and the first line of his obituary said it all: 'Roy Kinnear was a man who suffered fools gladly.'

Actors' obituaries, of course, are a different genre from 'Military' or 'Eccentric'. Like a critic on a first night, it's open season on actors after they've snuffed it. Some actors genuinely never read their reviews, and a lot more claim they don't. But here's the longest press notice you're ever going to get, and you're in no position to even pretend that you haven't read it.

Sneering at Stumpy was all very well, but at least he got his columns in the *Telegraph*. If I fell off a horse or a bar stool would any organ apart from *The Stage* even notice?

When I tell strangers what I do for a living, and after we have established that, no, they haven't seen me in anything, they will often share with me the revelation that acting is an insecure profession. There are only so many faces you can pull when confronted with such wisdom, so now I pop my eyes, slap a hand over my astonished mouth and gasp out how much I wish they had told me that thirty years ago.

Security, if you grew up in the sixties, was a word to mock. Approaching your sixties, the mocking rings a bit hollow. Most people who are going to abandon the theatre for saner professions will have done so before now, those of us who are still around have left it a bit late. More to the point, most of us would not want, under any circumstances, to do anything else.

On my fiftieth birthday, after a bumpy decade both personally and professionally, I had to admit, with as much candour as my ego would allow, that my career to date had fallen into two phases. Fifteen years of promise, followed by fifteen years of not quite fulfilling that promise. What would the third, and I suppose, final phase bring? Whatever it was, I was determined it was not going to taste sour. A bitter middle-aged actor is a very unedifying sight.

If patriotism is the final refuge of the scoundrel, then perhaps the one-man show is the last resort for the unfulfilled actor. Apart from the few busy and prosperous players who take it on for the challenge or from pure dedication to the subject, most of us on the solo circuit started because we were not being offered anything else sufficiently interesting to do.

We can take heart that that can happen to anyone, at any stage in their career. John Gielgud, like that great patriot Winston Churchill, had to live through his wilderness years. His response to a dwindling career in the 1950s was to tour a one-man show called *Ages of Man*: an anthology of great speeches reprising his unmatchable career as a Shakespearean actor. On a bare stage, dressed in a dinner jacket, he relived his former triumphs in that unique voice, described so beautifully as a silver trumpet muffled in silk.

If he had expired after that nostalgic retrospective, how those obituaries would have harped on his failure to move with the times. But, of course, he thwarted them all by re-inventing himself as a daring interpreter of modern drama, a much-sought-after guest star on film and TV, who went on working well into his nineties.

My more modest ambition was to try and thwart *The Stage* from memorialising me as ' . . . best known for his work on *The Archers*, radio's longest-running soap opera.'

From Ambridge to Africa

I hate to be disloyal about *The Archers*, partly because I know there are people who would make a wax effigy of my person, and pierce it repeatedly with a bare bodkin. And partly because Ambridge was good to me. I joined the cast just before the programme's twenty-fifth birthday and was asked to leave just before its fiftieth. Comparing photos of the two anniversary parties is a horrible witness to the ravages of time.

Over the years, I played three regular running characters and assorted cameos, including an absurdly fruity-voiced Bishop of Borchester in one episode, when I was all of twenty-nine. By then I'd been listening to the show for two decades, almost as long as I'd wanted to be an actor, but I'd be lying if I said that I was fulfilling a professional ambition. It was more a sort of fan's fantasy. Even in short trousers I could recognise terrible acting when I heard it, and in those days the acting (with honourable exceptions) was spectacularly awful. Too many of the cast were not actors at all, but more or less approximations of the people they played. Great accents, but that was about it.

One of those honourable exceptions was an actor called George Woolley, who for years played the character of Joby Woodford, husband of Martha, who ran the local shop. Joby was a deep-voiced, salt-of-the-earth countryman, all measured words and folkloric wisdom. George was a witty, wise and generous man in his seventies, one of a vanished breed of provincial actors, an ex-hoofer and very handsome juvenile in his time, whose career had been in the reps of the North and Midlands. The sight of him standing at the microphone, immaculately dressed in pastel shades, his day make-up no more than a subtle foundation, script in one hand while the other lightly patted the blue rinse of his wound-around hair, his growling, bucolic tones transporting his listeners to a homely country cottage, is a testament to the magic of radio.

I kicked off in *The Archers* as Mike Tucker, a bolshie cowman who seemed to be fighting a one-man class war in the feudal environs of Ambridge. It was fun, it paid, albeit BBC money, and didn't interfere too much with what, with the snobbishness of youth, I thought of as proper work. For me in those days, proper work was going from rep to rep, like George Woolley, playing lots of parts and waiting to be spotted as a great classical actor in the making.

Theatre directors were usually very accommodating about my fitting in recording sessions for *The Archers*. Most of them listened to the Sunday morning omnibus edition as a sort of alternative religious observance. I found, too, that it gave me a new kudos, even with people who hated the programme. Like one friend I had who would sit with his parents listening to the seven o'clock news on the radio every evening. As none of them could bear to hear *The Archers*, which always followed the bulletin, he would switch if off just before the theme music. The presenter always said: 'And now for *The Archers*, an everyday story of country folk . . . ' Tum-tee tum-tee tum-tee-tum. It amused him to time the switching off to a very precise moment: 'And now for *The Archers*, an everyday story of count . . . ' click. He claimed his parents never noticed.

Eventually, of course, a 'proper' job came up, which meant relinquishing the role of Mike Tucker to another actor, who incidentally is still playing it. I was sorry to go, but even I realised it was impractical to get to recordings in Birmingham from south of the Sahara.

*

'My dear, how would you like to play Romeo in Nigeria?'

Val West never made it to Head of the Drama and Dance Department at the British Council, but she should have. An attractively neat, birdlike woman then approaching fifty, she had given most of her working life to the Council and inspired a mixture of admiration and fear in her clients as well as in the diplomats she dealt with overseas. If that sounds a bit like obituary speak for 'a difficult cow', she wasn't. Just scrupulous, loyal and passionate about her work and the way she spent the British Council's money. There are a great many performers indebted to 'Auntie Val'. She never made any of us rich but we got to see some amazing places.

The deal was that one actor and one actress would adapt *Romeo and Juliet*, playing as many parts as possible and linking scenes and speeches with a commentary. It was a way of introducing African students to Shakespeare, which they had to study for their school exams. The places we were going to were too remote and the British Council too poor or too mean to send a full company so Val had come up with the 'Shakespeare Duo'.

'Are you sure it's possible, Val?'

'Well, Judi Dench managed it, dear.'

And she had. She'd made a particularly good impression in a ridiculously remote market town called Maiduguri near the Nigerian border with Chad, and I was sent back from there with a very smelly leather amulet for her from an admirer. I didn't realise that the leather wasn't cured properly, and in every African town we visited after that,

I kept changing hotel rooms because I was convinced mine always had a dead bush rat concealed somewhere.

'And who's going to be Juliet?'

'That's up to you, dear.'

'The director's going to let me choose my own Juliet?' A casting veto! Auntie Val had obviously spotted that potential which others seemed a bit slow to grasp.

'Director?'

'Yes, who's the director?'

'No, dear, it's just the two of you. Six weeks in Nigeria, two in Cameroon and a split week in Sierra Leone and the Côte d'Ivoire. Thirty-five pounds a week.'

I'd played Romeo before. Badly. Twice. The first time was as an amateur in Swansea, where in spite of being about the right age for the part, I had been acted off the stage by my Juliet. Eleanor Thomas, always known as Fanny, and I had started in the theatre at around the same time, and when Val phoned we were furthering our professional careers in Mother Goose at the Kenneth More Theatre in Ilford. From Prince of Darkness and Good Fairy back to Romeo and Juliet seemed like a good move to both of us. We fitted in bits of rehearsal between our entrances in the panto, and on the precious Sundays which were the only break from a twice-daily performance schedule.

'They'd like *Twelfth Night* too.' Val rang up one day between shows. 'I'll add a bit extra to the frocks budget.'

The 'frocks' were a series of silly and sillier hats, some sashes for the aristos, and an occasional chain or chunky ring. Given that English was never going to be our audience's first language, and we'd be performing in huge halls or even in the open-air, there was a tacit understanding that the performances would need to be, let's say, a little broader than usual.

Well, if they were broad before we left these shores, then by the time we came back they made our pantomime look infinitely subtle and nuanced. Fortunately, the only people ever to see them were the West African kids who found *anything* we did a lot more entertaining than reading Shakespeare to each other in a classroom.

Some of our friends told us that we were just colluding in post-colonial cultural imperialism. Others said that we would do anything to get somewhere warm in February. Guilty on both counts. Studying Eng. Lit. was certainly a hangover from the exam system left behind by the architects of Empire, and it doesn't get much warmer than the northernmost tip of Nigeria.

Our best defence was that we had Shakespeare on our side. His universality takes no account of imperialist motives or the weather. Every culture has its pompous and deluded spoilsports like Malvolio and likewise its star-crossed young lovers. The friends who thought we were just patronising never heard the gasps of hundreds of kids when Juliet stabs herself or the whoops of laughter when Malvolio appears in his yellow stockings. It's true that our performances in *Mother Goose* might have got similar reactions but the real revelation was what relish, what wonder, what fun they derived from Shakespeare's four-hundred-year-old language. Yes, they found it difficult. Doubly, trebly difficult for rural African youngsters who had never seen a play before, let alone bits of a play by Shakespeare. But they confronted the difficulty, and shared the rewards of their effort with us. They sometimes shared the lines too, chanting along with the passages they'd learnt by heart. If they were bored, they let you know it, but if they were having fun, the shows just took off. Silences were rare, but when a hush did fall, it was the most rewarding silence in the world. Performing to those students will be the nearest I get to knowing what Shakespeare's players must have felt on a first night at the Globe.

That first tour lasted for two months. Two months of bumping around in a Land Rover over red dirt roads, sharing slim rations with VSO teenagers teaching English or Science in their gap year, sleeping in Government Rest Houses furnished as if the last Colonial District Commissioner had just donned his sola topi and stepped off the veranda and into the bush.

Then there was the tedium of fifteen-hour road journeys after the scheduled twelve-seater prop plane hadn't shown up. The tannoy in the tiny fly-blown airport that eventually crackled into life and announced: 'Owin' to local conditions, the plane done disappoint.' The flies that hovered round your lips during the balcony scene as if they knew it would soon be your turn to open your mouth. The torn mosquito nets and the inevitable bites. The daily lunch of tinned sardines and sweet grey bread. That incubus that took up residence in your gut.

And the performances: fifty minutes of *Romeo and Juliet,* a quick can of fizzy orange and then fifty minutes of *Twelfth Night.* Back on the road and on to the next college. Evening shows where the electricity died, and you performed in the headlights of the Land Rover. Late nights spent in some wooden shack with a corrugated iron roof during a tropical storm, drinking local beer, listening to African pop music drowning out the rain, and the man from the British Council trying to talk Hausa to the legless locals.

I had never experienced a more memorable couple of months in my life than that first African tour. My love affair with Shakespeare was decades old, but my love affair with travel was just beginning; and I was discovering that I could combine the two passions and call it a 'proper' job.

*

Over the next few years the indefatigable Fanny and I strutted our stuff in eighteen countries all over Africa. When she couldn't face another two months of heat and dust, or being stuck with me for virtually twenty-four hours a day, I bullied another old friend, Holly Wilson, to take on her roles. They couldn't be less alike as people. Fanny, small, dark and very Welsh, a demon for saving on expenses and dressing for comfort, was a lot tougher than me and never succumbed to the bugs and fevers that reduced me to a pasty wreck. Holly, on the other hand, made me seem more robust, but whatever struck her down, she was always impeccable in performance and irrepressible at the nightly binges; tall, blonde and elegant she had more than a touch of the English Memsahib. What they both had in common was enormous talent, curiosity, and a life-saving sense of humour.

There wasn't much to laugh about in Mobuto's Zaire, or in Ethiopia under Mengistu or in Uganda just after Obote, where you locked a barred gate across your bedroom door and dived under the bed when you heard gunfire. The presence, in the midst of all this, of a couple of actors offering gems from the Bard only occasionally struck us as absurd. Most of the time we were having too much fun to think about it.

Some of the African experiences were so special as to seem almost unreal all these years later. But we really did visit the Sultan of Sokoto in his rambling palace made of red mud. Although his remote fiefdom was now one of many states in a modern Nigerian Federation, the Sultan retained an almost feudal power over his people as their religious leader, and it was a rare privilege to be granted an audience.

The meeting had been arranged by one of those indomitable English women who somehow manage to survive the privations of West Africa not just for weeks but for decades. Now in her sixties, Sonia had known His Highness since soon after independence and was evidently a regular visitor to the compound. She was as keen to show her familiarity with royal circles as we were to get a glimpse of his nibs, and the fact that not many actors passed through Sokoto, particularly in a professional capacity, must have made us seem as exotic to him as he was to us.

We were ushered into an enormous room with almost as many sofas as the Harrods' Depository they had evidently come from. Very dodgy wiring snaked from the walls to vast standard lamps, and the coffee tables and ornaments were straight out of *Country Life*. An enamel bucket was strategically placed in the centre of the room to catch the drips where the palace's mud roof had been jeopardised by recent rains.

After keeping us waiting for a suitably regal time, the Sultan arrived, flanked by two young men in immaculate indigo costumes and embroidered hats worn slightly at an angle. These were his sons, obviously agog to set eyes on an actress, that most louche type of Western female, actually there in their sitting room. (The week before, Fanny had made a strictly solo visit to the Emir of Kano's harem, where she chatted happily with his wives as videoed episodes of *Dallas* played on the giant TV screen.) Taking Sonia's lead, we stood until the Sultan had sat down, then tried to arrange ourselves in a suitably reverential yet comfortable position on a six-seater sofa with cushions like quicksand.

He seemed very ancient, his white head and beard covered almost entirely in what looked like a faded blue muslin scarf, which he somehow managed to keep floating over his lips even as he talked. He spoke very quietly in Hausa, which Sonia proudly and effortlessly translated for us. It was a monologue. Probably one he delivered to whomever Sonia had netted from the few new Brits who came her way. And it was fascinating.

His father had been Sultan when Lord Lugard led the British troops to capture his territory at the beginning of the century. He had been smuggled away in a rush basket to keep him out of the imperial clutches. 'Just like Moses,' Sonia improvised off-script, and the old boy nodded. It was obviously a rehearsed interruption.

He was more magnanimous than he needed to be about the intervening period of colonial rule, but his eyes lit up when he told us how he had succeeded to the Sultanate in time to see the British flag lowered in 1960. He honoured us with a little mime of a flag being run up, then a tiny shrug of the shoulders and the flag being lowered. He had witnessed the beginning and the end of the British Empire in his country, and the shrug just demonstrated what a tiny period those fifty-seven years amounted to in the history of his people. Then he stood up, and very courteously left the room with his two beaming boys. One of whom is presumably now the Sultan of Sokoto and maybe tells the same story about his father.

En route from Sokoto to Maiduguri, where Dame Judi had made such a hit, we skirted almost the entire northern border of Nigeria, playing in the major settlements at Gusau, Katsina, Nguru and Geidam but also stopping off at some more remote residential schools and villages to check up on how the VSOs were coping with their exacting living conditions.

Nearly every one of these intrepid youngsters bore gruesome scars on their knees and shins where they had regularly fallen from their motorised scooters onto the bumpy dirt roads. They lived in one- or two-roomed huts with only oil lamps or candles for light and a kerosene fridge. Tony Andrews, our tireless British Council officer, had loaded the Land Rover with bottles of Dettol for their weeping wounds and bottles of beer for their sagging spirits.

Our novelty value was such that, when we turned up to perform at a school, several hundred students from other schools would travel for hours to see us. They arrived in open-topped lorries so crowded that they had had to stand for the duration of the journey, often a couple of hundred kilometres. Apart from their unflagging enthusiasm, the real miracle was that they sprang from those rattling old trucks looking immaculate, their spotless white uniforms dazzling in the midday glare. This was very unfair because Fanny and I would invariably stagger from *our* vehicle looking like a couple of derelicts. It was the time of the harmattan, the dry relentless wind that plagues West Africa every winter, covering everything in its sandy dust. Standing, sweating in its inescapable embrace, I probably looked more like a puny terracotta warrior than the Romeo of those kids' imagination.

In that imagination I suspect they differed a lot from their European counterparts. Our version of doomed romantic love seems to have less resonance in a country like Nigeria – as we found out at one performance. It was during the tomb scene in the last act. Fanny lies prone on the wobbly school desks we had roped together to form her catafalque. As Romeo, I approach her body, unaware that she has feigned death in order that we can be reunited. Looking down at the corpse, I start to emote:

O my love, my wife!
Death that hath sucked the honey of thy breath,
Hath had no power yet upon thy beauty.

That morning, I had been vaguely aware of something dodgy about my pale breakfast omelette.

> Eyes, look your last!
> Arms take your last embrace ...

As I lift the lifeless body into my arms, the omelette decides
to assert itself.

> ... and lips, O you
> The doors of breath, seal with a righteous kiss
> A dateless bargain to engrossing death.

Fanny was about to get a kiss she would never forget, or
forgive. I ran offstage, through the open pass door and
threw up copiously and at length into a patch of scrub
grass. As Juliet was acting dead, there was very little Fanny
could do, and as the nauseous minutes passed, I could
hear a restless chatter starting in the audience. Someone,
who evidently hadn't got to the end of their text book,
started to applaud. Very quick-wittedly, Fanny raised
herself on one elbow, stretched her other arm in a waking
gesture and went straight back on script:

> Where is my lord?
> I do remember well where I should be
> And there I am. Where is my Romeo?'

The last line she spoke with such genuine vehemence that
she got an answer. But not from me. A voice halfway down
the hall gave Shakespeare's play an African conclusion.

'He think you dead!' the lad shouted. 'He gone find
another woman!'

*

Nigeria was regarded by the British Council, and doubtless still is, as a 'hardship posting'. So was our next stop, Cameroon. But when Fanny and I first arrived there, it seemed like Paris. Landing in the steamy port town of Douala on the south-west coast, we were whisked off to a splendid hotel, given ice-cold *citrons presses* and a miraculous dinner of *fruits de mer* and lobster. This was francophone Africa, where the colonisers had taught their servants to cook the French way. It was one legacy that French imperialism could be proud of, and the Cameroonian chefs had embraced it along with a Gallic pride and obsession with the quality of their food.

I'd heard vaguely of the Cameroons sometime during an inattentive school career but thought they were a range of Scottish mountains or a plate of small spoonerised almond cakes. In fact, it was a West African territory carved up between the French and the British which had even had German masters until the end of the First World War. In the singular, Cameroon is an independent state immediately south of Nigeria and is the most astonishingly beautiful country I have ever been to. A drive to the north-eastern part of the country, where we were to perform, is like the most intriguing geography textbook come to life: tea plantations, coffee plantations, rubber plantations. Jungle gave way to lush plateaux, which rose into grassy highlands and descended into dense forests.

The drive to Bamenda started at dawn and halfway there we were still in ex-French territory when we stopped for lunch. It was a typical dusty little village with open-fronted shops and a sprawling market, where the traders seemed to outnumber the customers and the flies outnumbered everything. Our driver stopped outside the only solid building in the main street, and we tipped out, aching from hours of swerving along potholed roads and not a little scratchy with each other after the endless confinement of the car.

An hour or so later, we emerged smiling, replete and just a little drunk. Here, in the middle of nowhere, the driver had been directed to take us to a real French bistro where the patron was an ancient ex-pat who was still importing his ingredients from France. We ate warm baguettes, drank chilled rosé from an earthenware jar and gorged on the most delicious local avocados and a wonderfully aromatic cassoulet of goat and enormous white beans. The patron apologised that his consignment of Perrier was late again. Who constituted his regular clientele we never found out.

The food in English-speaking Bamenda took us straight back to our penitential diet in Nigeria, but the town was welcoming and eccentric. The people speak a pidgin, rich in mangled English and French, and even the occasional German words from before the First World War. We were billeted on a British teacher who had been there for a decade and seemed unable to speak his own language properly any more, but his pidgin was an endless source of delight. One of his neighbours, a huge Cameroonian with a passion for Shakespeare, read me his translation of Hamlet's soliloquy, 'To be or not to be ...', which rendered 'The slings and arrows of outrageous fortune' as 'The sticks and the stones of the bad-luck man.'

*

Subsequent tours took us from the South African kingdoms of Lesotho and Swaziland to the benighted lands on both banks of the Congo river, from the sophistication of Tunis to the squalor of Kampala, from the confluence of the Blue and White Niles in Khartoum to the effluence of open drains in Kano. We drank unfiltered water and imported champagne. We ate oysters and we ate bush rat. We crossed rivers on leaky raft boats and travelled first class on the overnight train from Nairobi to Mombasa. We stood transfixed by the permanent rainbow over the thundering Victoria Falls, and stared shamefaced at the slums just yards from our windows in the Addis Ababa Hilton. And between gigs we had to fill in the time somehow; sliding along in a tiny canoe through the pristine Okovanga Delta in Botswana, peering at lions in a Zambian game park, water-skiing on a Zimbabwean lake, snorkelling off Mauritius and island-hopping in the Seychelles. It was tough.

A Rustic Revolution

Back in the real world, *The Archers* had taken me back to its bosom as Harry Booker, the Ambridge postman. I took the part over from an actor who had found a *proper*, proper job and given up acting altogether. I inherited his post bag, his Northern accent, and the captaincy of the Ambridge Wanderers football team. For someone born with two left feet, this last might have been a problem in any other medium but radio, and when the fictional team was challenged to a real match by the Worcestershire College for the Blind, I panicked briefly before inventing a pressing prior engagement. I wasn't there to see Ambridge lose, partly because the blind team was younger and fitter than ours, but also because they played with their own ball which had a bell in it.

Into its second half-century, *The Archers* now seems unassailable. Love it or hate it, the fact is that millions listen to it, and it has such a wide and influential constituency that even the ruthless and unsentimental Beeb would never dare to axe it. It wasn't always so, and in my second incarnation the programme seemed genuinely under threat. A new editor had taken over and brought with him a posse of new writers, mostly from television.

According to the powers that be, *The Archers* needed spicing up a bit and the first months of the new regime saw the sleepy rural idyll dragged into a twentieth century of sin and crime. And postmen weren't exempt. Harry acquired a new post bus to speed him on his rounds, and in my neighbourly way, I would offer lifts to the old folks of the village. On one occasion I had that Walter Gabriel in the back of my bus. For those not old enough to remember, Walter was the wily old geezer with a voice somewhere between a gargle and a constipated growl. His wheezing laugh and constant catchphrase – ' 'Ow do, me old pal, me old beauty?' – polarised the public's love-hate relationship with the show. He was also, after the eponymous patriarch and matriarch Dan and Doris, the programme's most famous character. So one day Walter and I were bowling along towards Borchester in my spanking new bus when he called to me from the back seat something like:

'Hey up, me old pal, me old beauty . . . who's that up ahead? And why be he a-standin' in the middle o' the road? Bit 'ot for a balaclava, ain't it?'

'You're right Walter! And what's that he's waving at us? Looks like a gun to me. (*Screeching of brakes.*) Walter, I think we're being hijacked!'

Tum-tee tum-tee tum-tee-tum . . .

And we *were* being hijacked (just like the programme). What happened next is not totally clear because I was rehearsing a play in Bristol during the next recording session and couldn't be in the following episode to explain all. I think we warranted a brief reference in The Bull along the lines of:

'What about that 'arry Booker bein' 'ijacked on his way to Borchester, then?'

'Aaagh, rum do. (*Pause.*) And have you heard about the gang-rape at Felpersham Women's Institute?'

Things may never have got to quite that pitch, but in the new fast-paced life of Ambridge, a hijacking was not much more of an event than a cow going into labour. It didn't last, of course, and before long, the village returned to the reassuring, if no less fictional, life of the caring country community.

However, the villagers soon found themselves without one pillar of their community. Harry Booker no longer turned up at coffee time with a postcard from Lilian in Guernsey or the team-list selection for next Saturday's match. I just stopped getting offered bookings. Years later, in one of the many spin-off books on the programme that ex-scriptwriters and producers churn out to earn a few bob, I discovered Harry had been promoted to Head Office in Borchester and taken his football boots with him.

Roots and Branching Out

If I hadn't been called Gareth, I doubt if the next job would have come my way.

A new company had started in Cardiff calling itself 'Theatre Wales', with a brief to employ only Welsh or Welsh-based personnel. I have an impeccable Welsh pedigree and a first name to prove it. 'Gareth', I'm told, means either 'Mighty Spear' or 'Gentle One', depending on who you're trying to impress.

It happened that nearly all the actors in that first season, including myself, lived outside Wales. Peeved local thespians, who had seen Theatre Wales as a potential employer, re-christened the new company 'Theatre 125' after the express train that brought us all in from Paddington.

The first season was beset with problems; the wrong choice of play, an inexperienced designer and one too many drunks. Wales has a reputation for producing hard-drinking actors and now, working with an exclusively Welsh cast for the first time, I realised why. Generations of Welsh actors came almost entirely from the working class, and that's what gave them their edge and their appeal. Acting for a living meant dressing up, putting on make-up, and talking posh; and that was no job for a real man, certainly not a real Welshman. Drinking too much reminded them what being a real man was like. It also made them an almighty pain in the ass.

There is no glorious heritage of professional theatre in Wales, and Theatre Wales wasn't about to change that image. During the second lacklustre season, I teamed up with a wonderfully eccentric man called Hugh Thomas and we founded a small-scale company called 'Made in Wales' to present new writing. I made a decision to swap from poacher to gamekeeper and drop acting for directing, at least for a while. In the fifteen or so years that I'd been acting, I'd played in most of the major regional theatres, as well as at the RSC and a couple of West End shows. Directors, it struck me, were often lazy, frequently misguided and usually had inflated egos. I really thought I could do better. Only when I'd been directing for a while did it strike me how many actors were lazy, misguided and had inflated egos.

Though Made In Wales never set the Severn on fire we were generally perceived as a 'good thing', and thanks to the tenacious directorship of our successor, Gilly Adams, the company survived almost to the end of the twentieth century.

There's a venue in Cardiff called the Sherman Theatre. It's a terrible name, following the American model of memorialising the money not the art. Mr Sherman had made his out of the football pools and offered the University of Wales a big chunk of it if they named a building after him. To his credit, the Vice-Chancellor chose to build a theatre. It is as well he has that to his credit, as a few years later the university found itself ten million pounds in debt and the theatre had to be sold off.

After a couple of years, the notoriously fickle Welsh Arts Council pulled the plug on Theatre Wales and offered a new franchise to a company that might claim to do better. Such a company needed to be building-based and the only suitable building was the Sherman. It was run at that time by Geoffrey Axworthy, a thoroughly decent man, without an ounce of malice and an admirable sense of fair play. Quite the wrong person to be running a theatre. He also

demonstrated a worrying lack of self-awareness by wearing a wig you could spot from across the Bristol Channel.
It used to slip over his eyes when he nodded off during
performances, which he invariably did, and it was rumoured
that when his first wife died, he traded it in briefly for a
black one to go to the funeral.

Geoffrey recruited me and a talented composer and
writer called Mike James to join him and form a trio of
directors to apply for the new Welsh Arts Council franchise. We won. I'm pretty sure it was a put-up job, Wales is
like that, but for the next three years I had a fascinating
time with the Sherman Theatre Company, directing a
repertoire of Shakespeare, new plays, revivals and my only
attempt at a musical.

I even managed to combine my two passions. Auntie
Val agreed to send the company to East Africa with a production of *A Midsummer Night's Dream*, and I invited
Anthony Cornish, an expert on the play, to direct it. That
gave me the chance to go back to Africa and perform with
both my Shakespeare Duo leading ladies, Fanny and Holly,
at the same time.

Everything went splendidly until we got to Lusaka, the
capital of Zambia. In the theatre bar one night, a bunch of
English accountants were getting loudly drunk and, not
surprisingly I suppose, were mistaken for us touring actors.
They played along and said that the next stop for the play
was South Africa where they were going to show the Zulus
how to do Shakespeare.

It was a stupid prank, but politically this was a very
sensitive time. It was during the last desperate years of
apartheid, and there had just been a fatal border incident
at Livingstone, where South African soldiers in disguise
had murdered some young Zambians. And, of course, at
that time there was a cultural boycott operating against

South Africa. There was no way we would have been working there.

Unfortunately, a white teacher who happened to be in the bar believed the fiction. I was midway through a beautiful speech of Oberon's –

> But we are spirits of another sort.
> I with the morning's love have oft made sport,
> And, like a forester, the groves may tread . . .

– when someone stood up in the auditorium and shouted: 'We must stop this performance!' It was the teacher.

> Even till the eastern gate, all fiery red,
> Opening on Neptune with fair blessed beams,
> Turns into yellow gold his . . .

'We must boycott this play. These people are going from here to perform for the fascists in South Africa!'

Suddenly the lights came on, and there were several tall figures standing by the exit doors. Our over-zealous teacher had informed the Home Secretary, who had sent his heavies in for a showdown. They started to walk down the aisles, guns slung over their shoulders.

Anthony Cornish, doubling as tour manager as well as director, rushed onstage to protest our innocence. The British Council, he told the audience, would never sanction a visit to South Africa; Equity, our union, forbade it; and none of the company would contemplate working there.

It was to no avail. We were told to get changed, go back to our hotel to pack and be out of the country by midnight. We were to be deported for consorting with the South African regime. After an abortive dash to the airport, where we found every outbound flight full, we were taken back into the city, put up in 'safe' houses and given large Scotches.

By this time, of course, the truth had come out. Next day we were back by the hotel pool and the following night back onstage. The accountants were given a good ticking-off, their firm were persuaded to make a 'voluntary' contribution to the Lusaka Playhouse and we gave an extra performance to raise funds for the victims of the Livingstone atrocity.

Kenneth Kaunda, the first President of Zambia, accepted the funds we'd raised from the British High Commissioner on the TV news and sacked his Home Secretary. Very appositely he concluded in the newspaper that: 'He has not performed well.'

Going back to Cardiff seemed a bit tame after that. Not that there was any shortage of crises there too. The news of the Vice-Chancellor's bad housekeeping had got out and the theatre was under threat of closure. The next year was spent in endless board meetings, organising fund-raising concerts, schmoozing with reluctant sponsors, standing at the exits shaking plastic buckets and frantically trimming budgets. I am hopeless at all those things.

Once the Welsh Office had been shamed into stepping in and buying the Sherman for the nation, I began to feel it was time to move on again. My coming birthday was my fortieth and the next decade was to bring me more sadness and ultimately more fulfilment than I'd ever known.

Steve

Back on the side of the Severn Bridge where the tolls are collected, work was very thin on the ground. I had always subsidised my theatre work with voice-overs (or voices-over, as one pedantic agent used to call them) but this is a world where to be out of circulation is to be dead. After five years away, I was dust.

I did some freelance directing, and some totally forgettable bits of TV. I spent seven interminable days recording a pronunciation dictionary for a CD-ROM where the only excitement came as you reached the letter 'F' and could look forward to the prospect of being paid to say 'fuck' in a posh voice into the microphone. Eventually I found a cosy temporary home at the BBC World Service. They have a department there called 'BBC English', but back in the nineties it was still called 'English by Radio', or 'E. by R.' and, inevitably, 'Ee by Gum'. It is one of the Corporation's best-kept secrets, except to the tens of millions who have learnt and still learn English on that frequency.

The department works out of Bush House, the most characterful and friendly of the Beeb's many mansions. It is staffed by dedicated producers and assistants and has a small core of actors on short-term contracts who provide the English voices for bilingual teaching programmes in a score and more of languages. As a member of the BBC English by Radio Repertory Company, you were like an eavesdropper at the Tower of Babel. You also met fascinating people from countries you'd never heard of, new countries carved out of old countries, people who had stories of enormous courage and people who you suspected had some pretty dodgy connections. You could chat to them over a subsidised meal in the canteen, share a drink in the venerable BBC club, marvel at their command of your own language, and take home something approaching a living wage. But as an actor, you joined the living dead.

I have never worked for more appreciative people or in such an unpressured atmosphere, but every day of my contract diminished my identity as an actor. Acting should engage every part of you, not just your brain and your voice, but your imagination and your capacity to take risks. Only the voice, speaking very slowly and clearly, and the little bit of the brain that remembers how to say 'Goodbye' in a dozen different languages were required at BBC English. So at least parting from a Romanian or a Sri Lankan now holds no fear for me.

*

What I really wanted was to be asked to join the National Theatre or go back to the Royal Shakespeare Company. In the mid-seventies, I'd had a truly undistinguished year with the RSC, playing the sort of parts that no actor would park on a double-yellow line for, let alone kill. I was Fenton, the dreary juvenile, in *The Merry Wives of Windsor*, and Earl Grey, that insipid infusion, in a crazy production of *Richard III* set in a sanatorium where we fought the Battle of Bosworth with sheets and pillowslips. In Ben Kingsley's wonderful *Hamlet* I managed only to land Rosencrantz and doubled as the petulant Priest who buries Ophelia.

That production was by a brilliant young director in her late twenties who rehearsed us for ten weeks in a corrugated-iron-roofed hut in Stratford called The Other

Place during the hottest summer anyone could remember. She was inspirational. She was dazzlingly clever. She was profoundly serious. After the play's opening night, when we all knew we were in an important success, she went home, wrote a letter and, with a combination of drink and drugs, killed herself.

Buzz Goodbody taught me a huge amount about Shakespeare, but she also taught me how lucky I was to have been born with a sizeable capacity for silliness. Which, as the great Alan Bennett observes, is not necessarily to be confused with foolishness.

I must have made no impression at all on the powers that be at Stratford, or maybe they thought I was *too* silly, because I was never asked back. I left the company, disillusioned and boasting only two achievements: I had learnt to drive, and I had met the love of my life.

The RSC is traditionally a very heterosexual company: actors being hearty in the pub, or wheeling prams along the banks of the Avon. During my season, out of a company of over forty actors, only two were gay. But it wasn't the solitary other one that I fell for, it was a stage-hand. Nobody, least of all myself, would have predicted that Steve and I would spend the best part of the next twenty years together.

By training, Steve was a gardener but potting up and pricking out for the Colonel's lady up at the Manor was a lot less lucrative than the overtime a unionised day man could get humping scenery at the theatre. He took a lot of persuading, when we moved back to London together, that being a landscape gardener there was as prestigious as being a plastic surgeon and even more sought after. The only time a film director ever called my home number was when Joseph Losey phoned to plead for Steve to make over his garden in Chelsea.

Perversely, the harmony Steve and I achieved together was largely because we had so little in common, and approached life and living in totally different ways. This was not unrelated to the differences in our chosen professions. Being a good gardener, Steve was patient, philosophical and calm. He was also totally uncompetitive in professional and social situations. None of these qualities, alas, typifies any actor I know. He was baffled by my obsessive need to work in the theatre, my bitterness at not getting a job and my jealousy of whoever did get it. I found it hard to understand why he didn't cultivate richer clients, charge more for his expertise, and just occasionally blow his own trumpet. Once we agreed to differ on such matters, we lived very happily as two sides of the same coin. It took me far too long to recognise that his approach was wiser, saner, and more conducive to a sweet life.

In spite of a dauntingly enquiring mind, and an elephantine memory, Steve had virtually no professional or academic qualifications. He mostly worked alone, except for the frenetic presence of our Welsh border collie, Meg. Eventually, in his early forties, he conceded that he needed more stimulus to fulfil the potential that everyone saw in his work, and he applied to take a degree in Landscape Architecture at university. He was accepted unconditionally. In the same month, he was diagnosed as HIV positive.

On the day Steve started his university course, I left him to go and work in America for the first time. The opportunity came at a time when I knew Steve's illness would soon enough change my life forever and end his. HIV is the prelude to AIDS, and in those days it was quite simply a death sentence. How long the process would take was the main question and whether or not I should leave him, if only for a couple of months, was the other.

I went. I can never regret the experience, but to be met at the airport on my return by Steve, half his normal weight and already suffering the symptomatic diseases that would kill him, made me thoroughly ashamed of myself. I swore I would never leave him again, and I didn't.

*

The BBC unknowingly came to our rescue in the last year of Steve's life by offering me a contract with the Radio Drama Company. If you ever listen to plays on Radio Four and think you keep hearing the same actors' names mentioned towards the bottom of the cast list, you can be fairly sure you're right: they're members of the RDC. It's shrunk now to a mere shadow of its former self, but for decades it was a refuge for actors who love doing radio, actors who are not being offered any other work, actors who are too lazy or frightened to get up on a stage, or for an actor like me who had just been reluctantly cast in another role. In my case, as a carer.

Thanks to the Beeb I was able to do both jobs simultaneously. I had done a stint on the RDC when I was a much younger actor, one of those who loved radio *and* wasn't being offered any other work. In those days it was called the Radio Drama Repertory Company, but some bright spark decided that the word 'repertory' had a whiff of the provinces about it, so the name had been changed. And that was the least of it. Years before, it had been a cosy doddle of a job, but the new broom at the Corporation had brought in 'the suits' to rationalise actors just like everything else.

Occasionally, 'a suit' would even come to a recording, and ask the toilers for 'feedback'. One actor took the opportunity to point out that the new work methods meant there was no time to rehearse a play properly before committing it to tape. He was met with puzzled incomprehension.

'If I employ a plumber,' the suit said, 'to change a washer, I don't expect him to have to 'rehearse' it in my time.'

The BBC was rife with such real and apocryphal stories, and the atmosphere was rank. But one thing hadn't changed, at least not by then. Although Steve had round-the-clock carers in our flat, there were times when I needed and wanted to be with him, and the moment came when I had to tell my employers the situation at home. Their response showed how a huge organisation could still be both practical and compassionate. Producers let me understand that even under the tight new regime they would somehow work round me if the need arose, they offered to suspend my contract and resume it when I chose, they gave me exactly the right level of support to make me feel I could still do my job properly. Both jobs.

Within a matter of days, I was to lose them both. Steve's condition deteriorated and I asked to be released from my contract so we could spend what time he had left together. It was just a couple of weeks.

We were living in Shepherd's Bush in the west London borough of Hammersmith and Fulham, and if you had to have AIDS, there was probably nowhere in the entire world where you would be better looked after. That, the love of exceptional friends and Steve's unbelievable courage somehow took us through to a dignified and peaceful end. That is a glib and completely inadequate way to describe those months, but it has to be enough.

Last-Chance Saloon

After the relief of Steve's death, I thought, like a lot of other people in that situation, that everything would change. I would move house, make new career decisions, get God, go to the dogs, do something worthwhile with my life. Nothing of the sort. I stayed put, cherishing and cherished by the friends who had seen me through the last two years, and scrabbled about for bits of work. Since my globe-trotting had been suspended now for a respectable period, I started to re-establish my voice-over contacts and moved about in that easy-going world for a while, waiting for someone or something else to change the direction of my life.

Shakespeare to the rescue once more. I got to play Richard III at last. By accident. It was Laurence Olivier's performance in the 1955 film that sealed my fate. I was seven years old when I first saw it, and from that day I fell irredeemably in love with the part, the player and the playwright. The Derby Playhouse had a jinxed production in its repertoire, where the previous two actors playing him had not, for different reasons, finished the run. You can't get proud about being third choice with a part like that on offer, so with just two weeks rehearsal I got to be the third Richard III, in a very dynamic production by Mark Clements, and play the role which had bewitched me since childhood. In the circumstances, I am sure mine was a pretty superficial reading of the part, but just getting through it gave me a huge confidence boost, and an indecent amount of fun.

There was a message on my answering machine when I got back from Derby asking me to ring *The Archers* office in Birmingham. For the third and, I suppose, last time I was being invited back to Ambridge as a regular character. But he was not to be a regular guy, and I was about to pass into 'soap' history.

Sean Myerson was the first openly gay character to speak in radio's longest-running soap. There had been a character called Shane, who worked at the wine bar, and was spoken of with wry amusement and references to the excellence of his quiche. Since real men don't even eat quiche, the listeners could draw their own conclusions, but Shane never uttered. Now the existence of the rural homosexual was to be acknowledged.

Everyone in *The Archers* has to sign a sort of Official Secrets Act promising not to divulge storylines, and it was made clear to me that I should keep Sean's sexual preferences a secret until the official 'outing'. The team decided that there would be no obvious giveaways. I was gradually insinuated into village life. Before I made my entrance, it was well known around the village that I was invaluable to the cricket team, lent a muscular hand at village functions and was somewhat fancied by the resident matrons. I ran, with my partner Peter, the rival pub to the village's famous watering hole, The Bull, a former roughhouse called The Cat and Fiddle. Hang on, what was that about a partner ...?

If we are all, as Andy Warhol said, going to be famous for fifteen minutes, an episode of *The Archers* might have been tailor-made to fulfil his prophecy. When they broadcast the revelation that Sean was gay, I imagined a torrent of Leviticus-quoting homophobes projecting me to instant but brief media fame. It never happened. On the same day as the broadcast, the TV soap *Brookside* showed an incestuous embrace between a brother and sister in the suburbs of Liverpool. By comparison, a cosy gay couple living in a country pub seemed entirely unremarkable and was barely noted.

In the event, Sean's appearances were also fairly infrequent. The writers, having been instructed to create the monster, had no idea what to do with him. Sean was not to be stereotypical, so I worked as a painter and decorator with a good eye for colour, rather than as an interior designer. I was unfailingly generous and good hearted; I'd lend my ladder to anyone. On the cricket field I was always the gentleman and eventually captained the village team to a glorious victory, crowned with a rousing speech in my pub when I was cheered to the echo.

But where was the partner, Peter? He was spoken of warmly by all, but he never served in our saloon bar. It might just have been budgetary constraints that meant there were never two homosexuals in the same episode, but I can't help feeling that, at that time, a Sunday morning conversation in bed over coffee and the papers would have been an Ambridge too far. Seven years later, there is a very credible gay couple in the programme, whose first broadcast kiss had most listeners thrilling to their romance.

I only had one real storyline, which was rather ill advised. I can say that because it was my idea. I suggested that Sean should attend the annual Gay Pride March in London. What upset listeners was that my attendance at that march was given more coverage than a protest march about the crisis in the countryside at about the same time. But Sean's absence from the village meant his missing a vital cricket match, which brought him into conflict with the only villager who seemed to have a problem with Sean's sexuality: my rival pub landlord, Sid Perks of The Bull. Some strongish scenes between us were the only opportunity I ever got to be anything other than anodyne.

Finding the Plot

You are more easily forgiven for being too young in a part than you are for being too old, but the torture it must have been to sit through my King Lear is barely imaginable. I was nineteen at the time and re-sitting my unsatisfactory A Levels at Swansea Grammar School. I thought I was marvellous and also rather gracious to have agreed to perform in the annual school play at all. Because by then I was a veteran Shakespearean performer, had already trod the hallowed boards of the Old Vic and the Royal Court and, before the age of twenty-one, had no doubt astonished London audiences as King Henry IV in *Henry IV*, King Richard II in *Richard II* and Macbeth in the play of that name. I was reviewed, sometimes even favourably, by the national press and was interviewed and photographed in *Vogue*, not to mention the *Swansea Evening Post*. In terms of career and celebrity, it has been downhill ever since.

The National Youth Theatre is a truly remarkable organisation. The vision of one man, Michael Croft, it has changed the lives of thousands of young people over a period of nearly fifty years. As an English teacher at Alleyn's School in south London, Croft had been inspired by the enthusiasm of his pupils for performing Shakespeare to set up a scheme that would rehearse and play through the long summer holidays.

The Youth Theatre grew into a national organisation, and, by the time I was sixteen, the minimum joining age, it was casting its net as far as South Wales. It was sponsored and promoted in those days by the *Daily Mail*, which was read by the only Tory in my immediate family, Auntie Dilys. A childless widow, regarded by all her nephews and nieces with a loving respect, she was the first and only person in my family to think that my obsession with acting was anything more than a phase. In the teeth of my father's passive disapproval, she cut out the application form from the paper and we sent it off.

Bristol was the nearest city to hold auditions, and after two nail-biting interviews I was accepted: to carry a spear and understudy in *Troilus and Cressida* at the Old Vic. It was 1964, I was sixteen and about to spend my first summer in London.

In those days, the National Theatre building had not yet been inflicted on the South Bank, so Sir Laurence Olivier, the first artistic director, and his company were temporarily resident at the Vic. Every day I rubbed shoulders with people who knew him, worked with him, and served him in the canteen, where, next to the checkout, was a cigarette machine that sold a now-defunct brand called 'Olivier'. I started smoking.

Kind cousins, part of the vast London-Welsh diaspora, took me in for the first summer and were wonderfully tolerant of my odd hours, my arriving home with the milkman, and occasionally not even then. My absences were wholly innocent, a missed last tube train meaning I had to crash out on someone's floor.

Five years later, I was an NYT stalwart, had graduated to leading roles, and was renting a two-bedroom flat with eight other actors. We took it in turns to use the beds, very chastely and, of course, changing the sheets on a fortnightly basis whether they needed it or not. In the evenings, I worked in a pub to supplement the cash I had managed to save from my university grant, and lived on four hours' sleep a night and a diet which precluded anything unfried. Theatre has never been quite such fun again.

What those wonderful summers really gave me, apart from acne and bags under my eyes, was an invaluable relationship with Shakespeare. Michael Croft was a great teacher and had what I suppose could be called a muscular approach to the plays. There was never much analysis but, instead, a shared conviction that if you spoke the verse loud enough, fast enough and with the right emphases, everyone, including yourself, would know what you were on about. It may have been a bit simplistic but just to have learnt so much Shakespeare, to have spoken it aloud in big theatres to full and boisterous young audiences takes away the fear, and replaces it with a love just this side of idolatry. The canvas of my professional life has, I suppose, been fairly small, but my palette has always had Shakespeare as its primary colour and the pictures are vivid and unforgettable.

One compensation of middle age is that it releases you from the soppier juvenile roles. Of course, the options diminish too. Having got Richard III and, very recently Macbeth, on an American tour, out of my system, the wish list was thinning out as inexorably as my hair. With the beard I had grown to play Macbeth, I was now looking unnervingly like Salman Rushdie. Since at that time he had a fatwa against him, I decided that the beard must go.

'How about Shylock in the autumn?' I put the razor down. Jonathan Church was absurdly young, at twenty-four, to be running a theatre but he had already rescued Salisbury from a very unhappy period in its history. The previous regime had been seen by many as a disaster; at first, putting on plays that nobody in Salisbury wanted to see and then capitulating by doing plays that someone might want to see, but not doing them well. Jonathan turned that around in a matter of months and found a way to please the conservative Wiltshire audience and still stage imaginative and excellent work. We had worked together on David Mamet's explosive play of sexual politics, *Oleanna*, where I had played opposite a terrific actress called Carolyn Backhouse. Now we were going to play Portia and Shylock in the first play of Jonathan's 1997 season.

The Merchant of Venice is the Shakespeare play most likely to offend cultural sensibilities. Plenty of his other plays can offend political sensibilities. On one of our Shakespeare Duo tours of Africa there was unease from the communist junta then in power in Ethiopia that we would enact the murder of King Duncan, or at least the scene between the Macbeths moments after they have done the deed. It was not so long since that regime had murdered their own now-sainted Emperor Haile Selassie in not dissimilar circumstances. In the event, the scene was sneaked in during a mixed programme of scenes billed as 'Snipets (sic) from Shakespeare' and elicited more applause than our performances deserved. After four hundred years, Shakespeare can still snipe very effectively from the sidelines.

But in the land of the free, the First Amendment to the American Constitution could not prevent cities in Michigan and New York State from banning *The Merchant of Venice*, nor the New York School Board from forbidding the play on the grounds that it might foster anti-Jewish feeling. Performances have been placarded, barracked, and boycotted. Especially in the United States, theatre managements are nervous: wealthy patrons might threaten to withdraw their patronage if the play is programmed.

The imputation of anti-Semitism has stalked the play for well over a century, and it has caused pain and anguish amongst students, academics and audiences, all alarmed to contemplate that the author they worship above all others might have been a Jew-hater. The Nazis certainly thought he was. They encouraged productions of the play throughout the Reich during the thirties and the war years, and in Vienna, the Gauleiter commanded a performance of it on the grounds that 'every Jew active in Europe is a danger to European culture.'

Plenty of my Jewish contemporaries have told me the memories they have of studying *The Merchant* in a classroom full of Gentile classmates who saw the play as undeniably a clash between Christian heroes and a Jewish villain. Often the solitary representative of their race, they would be asked to play Shylock in class readings: their unease remains with them today. Seeing the play in performance could be equally uncomfortable.

I suspect the number of Jews who saw me play Shylock in Salisbury could be counted on the fingers of one hand. Wiltshire has a small Jewish community in Swindon, but the county has no synagogue, and many of our Protestant middle-aged and middle-class audience would have been puzzled at the controversy the play provokes on the other side of the Atlantic. How can the text be controversial: isn't it Shakespeare?

Controversy would much more likely centre on the style of production. Anything not in ruffs and farthingales might arouse suspicion, but although Jonathan's production was relocated to a Victorian Venice, it was admirably unfussy. Venice was dark, moody and wet and contrasted with a dignified Belmont of light and pastoral optimism.

It's rare for a modern director not to have a strong agenda when staging any Shakespeare play, it is the curse that comes with a familiar repertoire. To approach *The Merchant of Venice* with anything like an open mind smacks of laziness or naivety. I would not accuse Jonathan of either, but there were no directorial theses on the evils of capitalism or the universality of racism; we got on with telling the story of the play. It's a mistake to think that Shakespeare's plots are somehow programmed into the national psyche. They are not, and you can alienate an audience if you assume they are.

The play is categorised as a comedy; more correctly, I suppose, a romantic comedy. The main plot is the love story between Portia, the lady of Belmont, and her impecunious suitor, Bassanio. She is bound by the terms of her father's will to marry only the man who passes a test by choosing correctly from three caskets, one of lead, one of silver and one of gold. Being rich, and as Bassanio swiftly adds, beautiful with it, she is much sought after. There are comic scenes where international suitors come and choose first the gold and second the silver and are banished to a lifetime's celibacy. Bassanio, of course, gets it right by choosing the least flashy option, they marry and, after overcoming some little local difficulties, look like living happily ever after.

A plot almost worthy of opera in its silliness, and mostly stolen, like so many of Shakespeare's plots, from an Italian original. In this case part of a fourteenth-century epic fairy tale, called *Il Pecorone*. From that original also comes the subplot of the Jewish moneylender. In order to finance those expensive trips to Belmont, our romantic hero needs to borrow money and he approaches his godfather, who in turn solicits a usurer. As a bond, the moneylender suggests a pound of flesh instead of the usual interest, and the deal is struck. When the debt becomes due, our hero is too busy enjoying himself in Belmont to remember the date, and when he turns up late in Venice, the moneylender refuses the cash and insists on the fleshy option instead.

The case comes to court and things are looking grim, when the lady of Belmont arrives disguised as a lawyer.

He/she argues that the moneylender can have his pound of flesh, but as there is no mention of blood in the bond he must not spill a drop when exacting his forfeit. Thwarted! The usurer tears up the bond and storms off.

As the bare bones of *The Merchant of Venice*, this is obviously Shakespeare's source, but, of course, he introduces other subplots and themes and whereas *Il Pecorone* never even gives the Jewish moneylender a name, Shakespeare creates his most controversial character and calls him Shylock.

In New York I once met a financier who, in the polite way of most Americans, even financiers, asked me what I was doing. I explained I was playing the part of Shylock. He looked blank, but when I started to explain, his glazed expression suddenly changed.

'Shylocking!' he said. 'Sure. We have a rival who's always trying to shylock us.'

To him it was a verb, and he was genuinely ignorant of its source. Shylock is a noun too, and shares the distinction of being one of only two Shakespearean characters to have entered the language that way. The other one is Romeo.

Was I going to make a better Shylock than I had a Romeo? That wouldn't be difficult. In my very late forties I was probably about the right age. Although there are references to 'old Shylock' in the script, they really only distinguish him from the youngsters who mostly inhabit the play. He could be any age old enough to have a teenage daughter. Surprisingly, there are no allusions to his physical appearance in the play. We know he wears a gabardine and has a beard because he talks of Antonio spitting on both, most graphically on the latter: 'you that did void your rheum upon my beard ... '

Everything said to or about him refers to his personality, not the way he looks. This really surprised me as I trawled the play for clues until I read about the way that Jews were represented onstage in Elizabethan and pre-Elizabethan times. They wore huge false noses and red-haired wigs. It was a tradition, like a king wearing a crown or a clown his motley. I could see where the idea for the big nose came from, it's a not unusual Semitic characteristic, but I couldn't recall seeing that many ginger-haired Jews. It is among the many myths that accumulate around the Bible narratives that Judas, who betrayed Jesus, was a natural redhead. If, as the Gospels suggest, the Jews as a people were responsible for Christ's betrayal and death, the association becomes obvious. Nobody in the play needs to describe Shylock the Jew because they all know he's the hook-nosed carrot-top.

Amazingly, that tradition lasted well into the nineteenth century, until the maverick Edmund Kean thought better of it. It was his Shylock that made Kean's reputation overnight, but even before him the part was a magnet for ambitious actors. There's no record of who first played it in Shakespeare's company at the Globe, and a natural assumption would be that it was the leading man, Richard Burbage. The actor-manager who created Richard III, Hamlet, Othello, Macbeth, King Lear and probably Prospero would have been an electrifying Shylock.

But Shylock is only in four of the play's twenty scenes; he disappears before the end of the fourth act on a lousy exit line:

> I pray you, give me leave to go from hence,
> I am not well, send the deed after me,
> And I will sign it.

And a count reveals that he speaks barely a quarter of Hamlet's lines. I think Burbage was much likelier to have been playing the hero, Bassanio. He's got the lion's share of the script, and he gets the girl. But I wonder if, after the first night, Burbage realised his mistake and made a grab for the big nose and the ginger wig.

Playing with Paranoia

I've been an actor just long enough to remember when regional repertory theatres had leading men and women, who played all the juicy parts in a season and had that reflected in their company status and in their wages. A combination of a more healthy democracy amongst actors and less cash amongst theatre companies has abolished both those distinctions. Everyone is now paid a company wage, so pitiful that non-theatre folk are simply incredulous that actors can live on it. They can't, of course.

My pittance at Salisbury was subsidised a bit by the odd trip up to Ambridge and the rail journeys to the studios in Birmingham were useful for learning lines and doing some research. There was no shortage of sources. It turns out more is written about Shylock than any other Shakespearean character apart from the ubiquitous Hamlet. He provokes as much passion in academics as he does in audiences and actors. Chapter upon chapter of textual analysis, psycho-analysis too. It was all fascinating, and faintly amusing to see how the same couplet could mean a dozen different things. Of course, all the theorising can certainly help to understand the character of Shylock, but by definition, only an actor playing the part can know what it's like to *be* Shylock. I decided to give my brain a rest from the scholars and see where instinct and the text would take me.

I love rehearsals, partly because the process of play-making still thrills me and partly because it is a period when actors get to know each other with an intensity that must be rare outside of a submarine or a prison cell. You can learn more in three weeks about the person playing your lover, brother, spouse than you might get to know about a next-door neighbour in forty years. It might not always be a harmonious relationship and it may end with the abruptness of death after the last night, but it will rarely have been boring.

This intimacy grows less during the actual rehearsal than during the coffee breaks, lunches or evenings in the pub. Exploring the feelings and reactions of your character in a play often merges into self-revelation, not necessarily about anything profound but no less telling for that. Over a pint, an actor might reveal to a virtual stranger in the company a part of his history or a personal detail that, in other circumstances, torture would not elicit.

When it came to our coffee breaks, I found myself in conversation only if I instigated it. The decisions of where to grab lunch or when to meet at the local seemed to be made without reference to me. There was no animosity or even coolness from the rest of the cast, just the absence of inclusion. A mild paranoia started to set in. Bad acting? Bad attitude? Bad breath? Were they all sitting in the pub accusing me of one or all of the above? I don't think I was fooling myself when I found the answer. It was Shylock.

He is the ultimate outsider, and that status somehow permeates his entire presence. When he's offstage, what we learn about him is what other people say, and it's never flattering. When he's onstage, people mostly talk at rather than to him. Shakespeare has somehow endowed the part with an essence of isolation, and I began to wonder if it was contagious.

We had two black actors in our cast. For them, living in Salisbury was a weird experience because, for the first time in their lives, the only black face each saw every day was the other. I don't think it was that the local population reacted to them differently but that their very exclusiveness made them regularly aware of difference. They were always quite glad to get back to London at the weekends.

Shylock must have felt a similar and more profound relief when he could return from his day's moneylending on the Rialto to his 'sober house' in the Venetian ghetto. Although Shakespeare never mentions it, and may not even have known about it, the first Jewish ghetto was in Venice: the Ghetto Nuovo, a district where metal found-ries were traditionally located. When I first visited Venice a couple of years later, the first thing I did was to take a slow, observant walk from the Rialto Bridge to the Jewish Ghetto. Shylock would likely have been moving more swiftly to get inside the ghetto's barred gates before the dusk curfew that confined Venice's Jews within its limits.

There, at least, he could live according to his laws and customs. Waiting for him at home, though not for much longer, would be his daughter Jessica. Although his wife Leah is mentioned in the play, the assumption is that she has died, maybe even in childbirth. So Jessica, as well as be-ing his only child, is also the only Jewish female character in Shakespeare. As the single parent of a teenage daughter, coming from an ethnic minority and living in a ghetto, it is hardly surprising that Shylock is a strict father. Hardly surprising, too, that Jessica is so resentful that she falls in love and elopes with a Gentile boy to escape his tyranny.

The household is completed by that most unfunny comic servant, Launcelot Gobbo. As a Christian, Gobbo is given plenty of opportunity to make fun of his master's racial and religious peculiarities, his miserliness and his control over Jessica. Even-handedly, Shakespeare leaves you in little doubt that Gobbo is a lazy, fat slob.

It's an intriguing ménage. But there is a fourth char-acter who would have had access to Shylock within the confines of his domestic life. Tubal, referred to by Shylock as 'a wealthy Hebrew of my Tribe', is the only other Jewish man in Shakespeare, a moneylender like Shylock and the only person in the play who shows any sympathy for him.

Tubal has only one scene, when he returns from an unsuccessful trip to Genoa where Shylock has sent him to retrieve his errant daughter and the loot she took with her.

In our Salisbury production, the part was played by Paul Blake, who also had Old Gobbo and the Duke of Venice waiting for him in the quick-change room backstage. It's a very crucial scene and during rehearsals, Paul was the actor I could most easily relate to both on and, maybe not coincidentally, off the stage. Our brief duologue became pivotal for me in Shylock's journey through the play.

Unfortunately, in performance I could never look at Paul. The designer had given him a suit of travelling clothes for the Genoan journey which included a huge, round fur hat straight out of *Doctor Zhivago*. Paul said it made him look as if he was 'peering through a yak's arse!' Any eye contact would have reduced us both to helpless and inappropriate mirth. The real importance of Tubal to me and to me as Shylock would emerge a lot later.

*

The show opened to good reviews and played to full houses. Once settled into the dressing room with my fellow players, I dismissed those earlier feelings of isolation as actor's paranoia and began to enjoy that intense and short-lived camaraderie peculiar to rep. I was sharing the dressing room with my arch enemies, Bassanio and Antonio, who are onstage a lot together, leaving me alone as I waited for my well-spaced scenes and, after my final exit from the trial scene, throughout the whole of the fifth act before the curtain call.

As a first-night present, I had been given a copy of John Gross's *Shylock – Four Hundred Years in the Life of a Legend*. More than once I heard the applause start for the end of the show and had to dash down three flights of stairs for the curtain call having got totally immersed in that fascinating book. Gross, a theatre critic as well as a scholar, writes thrillingly about the character's history, his impact on the life of the theatre and his place in the pantheon of great fictional enigmas. Among the performances he recalls was the one which had made the greatest impression on me as a student, Laurence Olivier's Shylock.

I am only one of dozens of actors of my generation who blame Laurence Olivier for their choice of careers. It's fashionable now, particularly amongst people who never saw him, to dismiss Olivier as a mere technician. Well, there was nothing mere about his technique. He was utterly mesmerising, and although I've seen other actors who have moved me more to laughter or to tears, I've never seen one to equal his magnetism and his daring onstage.

As a teenager, I had often hitch-hiked up from Swansea at weekends to gorge myself on theatre. If the lifts were lucky, I could make a two o'clock matinée at the Royal Court, a five o'clock show on Shaftesbury Avenue and race down to Waterloo in time to see whatever the fledgling National Theatre had to offer in their first home at the Old Vic. It didn't matter what was playing: I sat through some plays in their repertoire half-a-dozen times. If Olivier was in the show, you'd be very lucky to get a seat, but for next to nothing, you could stand at the back of the stalls, and that's where I witnessed his Othello, his James Tyrone in

A Long Day's Journey into Night, his Captain in Strind-
berg's *Dance of Death* and even the occasional cameo role
he played as part of the ensemble. Whatever he was playing, the stage simply lit up whenever he came on. And that
was no illusion. The lighting technician, by all accounts,
was primed to tweak up the intensity of light when Olivier
first entered.

Prince Charles threw a party at St James's Palace in 2001
to celebrate the Fiftieth Birthday of *The Archers.* I was no
longer in the programme by then, but long service must
have merited me an invitation. At the party there were
speeches from Beeb luminaries, a very funny cabaret and
then finally a speech by HRH. As he stepped up to the
podium, up went the lights. Royalty.

I went to see Olivier play Shylock five times, but only on
the last occasion did I actually see him onstage. It was at a
time when he was in very poor health and his understudy
went on for him more often than not. Poor Lewis Jones,
whom I worked with later, told me about the sinking feeling he got when the audience groaned their disappointment on hearing that Lewis would be playing Shylock
instead of Himself.

It's difficult for me to be objective about Olivier's
performance. I was, after all, still in love with him. This
production had, like ours in Salisbury, set the play in a
Victorian Venice with Olivier resembling a cross between
Disraeli and one of the Rothschilds. It was a dignified,
rather disdainful portrayal, and a far from villainous
reading of the part. Even so, it was a surprise to learn from
Gross's book that Olivier and his director, Jonathan
Miller, had cut some of Shylock's most infamous lines in
their attempt to make him more sympathetic, including
this speech:

I hate him for he is a Christian,
But more for that in low simplicity
He lends out money gratis, and brings down
The rate of usance here with us in Venice.
If I can catch him once upon the hip,
I will feed fat the ancient grudge I bear him . . . !

I couldn't help feeling in retrospect that that was cheating.

Olivier's performance is most famous for a moment which has nothing to do with Shakespeare's play. At the end of the trial scene, when Shylock has been thwarted in his plot to kill Antonio, deprived of half his fortune and told he must convert to Christianity, he leaves the stage. Olivier took a long time to exit. There was a lengthy pause, and then a heart-stopping cry of pain and anger offstage. Of course, I had read all the reviews and was expecting it, but it was still a chilling, thrilling coup nonetheless.

It's not so surprising that right up until the twentieth century, actor-managers would leave the romantic story of Portia and Bassanio unresolved and end the play with Shylock's exit.

*

In Miller's production, Bassanio was played by a striking young actor called Frank Barrie. Twenty years later he threw a pewter mug at my head, and I ducked. I really shouldn't have. It was during the banquet scene in *Macbeth* when Frank, to banish the blood-stained ghost of Banquo, would hurl his wine goblet towards me. At rehearsals, as the ghost, I had been fearless, but on the first performance, Frank's paranoia was so convincing that I felt sure real blood would get spilled, so I ducked. My spectral credentials vanished and I got a mighty laugh. In the interval, my apologies were very graciously received but I was left in no doubt that Frank would never have mistimed so crucial a piece of business.

We were in Tokyo at the start of an eccentric itinerary which had started in Oman and would end up in Iceland. Our troupe, The London Shakespeare Group, was a sort of halfway-house between the Shakespeare Duo and a full company; it was one of Auntie Val's last schemes before she retired from the British Council with her well-earned MBE.

Appropriately, the four founder members had all been blooded on the West African circuit: John Fraser and Suzan Farmer had competed with Gary Raymond and his wife Delena Kidd for the title: 'the Lunts of Lagos'.

When casting, this gang of four would rate personal compatibility as highly as talent so that most tours were a very rewarding romp; up to eight actors, in a clear, visually arresting production. The tireless Delena would promote the shows, emphasising the company's flexibility, and the economy achieved by an entire show that could be packed in a trio of large metal cases. In a hastily typed memo, she once sought to reassure an overseas promoter: 'The LSG, you will be pleased to know, travels with only three drunks.'

Halfway through our curious schedule, Frank, entirely sober, stepped from his hotel bath, slipped on the shiny marble floor and broke his knee. Whilst his leg was being encased in thigh-high plaster, I rashly offered to go on instead of him. I was barely out of my teens when I had last played Macbeth, and in the intervening years, not surprisingly, I had lost my once-perfect grasp of the lines. It was not my finest moment, and the next night, Frank was determinedly back playing the role – on crutches.

Unashamedly, Frank models himself on our mutual idol, Laurence Olivier, and I think he's the only person

I know more in thrall to him than I. Frank loves acting, and it's evident in everything he does, both on and off-stage. So his other hero, apart from Sir Laurence, seems an odd choice: the nineteenth–century actor William Charles Macready. Macready despised acting in spite of his being one of the most accomplished players of his day. The most shameful moment in his life, he declared, was when against his better judgement he allowed his children to witness him in performance.

Macready is a one-man show which Frank has performed for over a quarter of a century. Although I have seen it half-a-dozen times, it never fails to delight me. Apart from the qualities that any fine actor brings to a role, Frank has a rare and rather old-fashioned one in his armoury. Charm. And he uses it shamelessly and to magnificent effect.

The show has taken him all over the world and very often been his principal source of employment. During our tour, I asked him what every actor of his acquaintance must have done. How do I go about getting a solo show together? Is it, who do I look like? Or is it a question of finding someone who hasn't already been solo-ed?

'Wait till you feel a passion,' was all he would say.

PART TWO

The Shock of the Old

At the end of the run of *The Merchant* in Salisbury, Jonathan Church and I discussed the possibility of my coming back to direct a show, and we fixed on a slot in his programme several months ahead.

'So what have you got planned between now and then?' he asked me.

'I'm putting together a one-man show about Shylock,' I said, off the top of my head.

Jonathan didn't pause. 'Sounds good. I've got a slot next September in the studio theatre. Five or six performances?'

'Er . . . six. But . . . ?'

'Great!'

Off he went, leaving me that most ineluctable thing, a deadline. And that was really all I had, apart from the small stirrings of a passion.

Nobody I spoke to after Jonathan shared any of his jaunty confidence in the project, and that went for me too. I had not really asked myself what a one-man show about Shylock would give to an audience that they couldn't get from Shakespeare's play. I had found playing the part one of the most difficult and fascinating challenges I had ever undertaken, but why would that be of interest to anyone else?

Having no answer, I ignored the question for as long as I could by carrying on with my research. The plot, the sources of the story, the history of the play in performance were all easy meat. I had already done some superficial reading about the Venetian ghetto and how Jews were perceived in Shakespeare's time, but had no overall view of the people Shylock so singularly represents in the play.

I got hold of a coffee-table book about Jewish history and culture, a sort of Moses-to-Jackie Mason romp in twelve illustrated chapters. It was one of the most shocking books I have ever read, all the more so for its facile format. The Biblical bits I was familiar with from a chapel childhood, the Holocaust, of course, the late millennium entrepreneurs, scholars, scientists, artists. It was the two thousand years in between that took me by surprise, and what most shocked me was not so much what I learnt but the depth of my ignorance.

The extent and barbarity of European anti-Semitism from medieval times to halfway through the twentieth century was, I am ashamed to say, a revelation to me. I knew that Jews had become so unpopular at the end of the thirteenth century that they had been banished from England and were not permitted to return until after Oliver Cromwell's intervention nearly four hundred years later. For that reason, I knew, too, that Shakespeare was unlikely to have mixed with any openly Jewish people.

But the beating, burning and brutality that preceded the expulsion from England was news to me. So was the adoption of similar tactics by so many other European countries: France, Spain, Portugal. Venice, pragmatic throughout its history, turned out to have been a relatively tolerant city for the Jews, who kept the wheels of commerce in motion with their usury.

I began to think of the antagonism the other characters show towards Shylock as less a personal than an institutional racism. Even Tubal, the only other Jewish man in the play and who never speaks to anyone except Shylock, is introduced to the audience with a line of racial abuse:

'Here comes another of the tribe; a third cannot be matched, unless the devil himself turn Jew.'

I saw that my play would have to confront anti-Semitism in a larger context than that of the play. If my ignorance of Jewish history was in any way typical, then the audience should go on the same disturbing journey that I was undertaking.

From my potted history, I graduated to more detailed and more specific accounts. I had heard of 'The Blood Libel', the absurd myth that Jews kidnapped and killed young Christian children, and used their blood in religious rituals. But I had no idea that the first recorded instance had been in England in the twelfth century. A young skinner's apprentice called William had been found buried in a shallow grave in a wood near Norwich just before Easter. He had most likely died of disease or malnutrition but rumours started to spread that he had been abducted by some of the local Jewish community. As the rumours spread, so the details of his death grew more fanciful and more gruesome. He had, the story went, been crucified and afterwards his blood drained into bowls for the making of matzos, the unleavened bread eaten by Jews during the Passover. After a dignified re-interment by the monks, there were claims that little William had been responsible for recent miracles, and he achieved the status of a local saint.

In Holy Trinity church in the village of Loddon in Norfolk, I went to see a rather primitive painting on the rood-screen depicting little William's grisly end at the hand of his Jewish murderers. For those unable to read of his martyr's death, a permanent pictorial reminder is useful propaganda.

The vicar of Holy Trinity, Reverend Christopher Chapman, was quick to point out to me that the little leaflet outlining the history of his church draws attention to the painting as an example of the evils of demonisation. In the magnificent cathedral ten miles away in Norwich, where William's remains ended up in pride of place amongst the holy relics, there is nearby a small and peaceful Chapel of the Innocents, dedicated 'as a reminder of the persecution, suffering and countless innocent victims in every age and particularly in the twentieth century'.

The city of Lincoln was witness to perhaps the most famous English example of the Blood Libel, so famous that it is memorialised in Chaucer's *Canterbury Tales*. The last lines of *The Prioress's Tale* are:

> O yonge Hugh of Lyncoln, slayn also
> With cursed Jewes, as it is notable
> For it is but a litel whyle ago;
> Preye eek for us, we synful folk unstable
> That, of His mercy, God so merciable
> On us His grete mercy multiplye
> For reverence of his mooder Marye.
>   Amen.

I had arranged to meet a writer and amateur historian called Karen Gennard to show me Hugh's shrine in Lincoln Cathedral. There is hardly anything left of it; it was destroyed by Cromwell's men during the Civil War. But Karen showed me an architectural drawing made just before its destruction. Built with financing from King Edward I, who some years later expelled every Jew from England, it was hugely impressive and bore royal emblems to add to its importance. The perpetuation of the myth was obviously thought well worth it.

Karen gave me a brief history. On the last day of July 1255, an eight-year-old boy disappeared from his home in the city. A month later, his body was found in a well belonging to a Jew called Jopin who, presumably under torture, confessed to his murder. A huge conspiracy theory evolved, claiming that a countrywide network of Jews had agreed that a boy should be sacrificed in that city and his body kept until a Jewish gathering could supervise his crucifixion as a Paschal offering. Karen had researched several other versions of the story, some outlining the scourging, the crowning with thorns and the piercing with a spear to which little Hugh was subjected.

She was a relative newcomer to Lincoln, and had been told the story of Hugh's martyrdom by a schoolteacher she had befriended. According to Karen, the teacher told the tale as historical fact, making no concession to its obvious invention as anti-Semitic propaganda. Only when the story was over did Karen point out that she was Jewish. The two have not spoken since.

The Blood Libel served to fuel anti-Jewish feeling long after William of Norwich and Hugh of Lincoln. Throughout the following centuries there have been countless reports of ritual murder by Jews, canards which have found special credence in Eastern Europe. The last verified account was of forty Polish Jews killed because they had supposedly butchered a young Catholic child and used his blood in the making of unleavened bread. That was in June 1946.

Subliminally, the Blood Libel still lives on in popular culture today. The story of Eastern European Christians abducted by night, the blood drained from their bodies by those who hate the sight of the True Cross. Dracula.

Anti-Semitic myths are legion, and the origins of some have been more or less forgotten, even though we unwittingly use their titles. The Wandering Jew is of the genus *tradescantia*, and commonly cultivated in hanging baskets and window boxes. Gardeners are divided about its merits. The Wandering Jew is also a medieval legend that perpetuates the myth of the Jewish Christ-hater.

The story tells of a cobbler named Ahasuerus, who watched the procession as Christ was taken to be crucified. When Jesus paused to rest and leaned against the wall of Ahasueras' house the cobbler pushed Him away and told Him, He could not rest there and must keep moving. Christ responded by telling the man that although He would be moving on and would find rest, for Ahasueras there would be no rest. He was condemned to wander the earth until the end of time for insulting Jesus Christ.

Enter Tubal

I wove some of these legends into my script, along with the documented history, the extracts from Shakespeare and the anecdotage of the play in performance. There were certainly enough elements there now to make a full-length play, so I put together what I thought was a good working draft and rang Frank Barrie. Nobody knows more about the solo performer's relationship with an audience than Frank, and I was determined that he should direct the show.

He asked me over to his house in south London to read him the script. I had barely started before I began to feel like an undergraduate reading his cumbersome essay to a very patient don. I waded through the whole clumsy effort, losing heart with every page.

'I can see the research,' he said, 'but where's the play? There's nothing wrong with the ideas, but they need a context. If you're addressing the audience directly, we have to be comfortable with who you are. So, who are you? Are you Gareth? Are you Shylock? Are you the actor playing Shylock? You've got to find a voice.'

Whatever my qualities as a performer, I don't possess enough of Frank's characteristic and enviable charm to woo an audience as myself. If I was going to have the nerve to be the only performer in my own play, I would certainly need a character to hide behind. But what character? The notion of being an actor playing an actor struck me as just too – well – actorish.

If Shylock himself was to be my narrator, how could I credibly give him that approachability that would put the audience at their ease? Mine is a sympathetic account of the character, but it is not so dishonest as to pretend that Shylock is likeable. Also his lines in the play are so complex and so textured that any words I might put into his mouth would be merely bathetic.

For a few weeks, I despaired of finding my voice. I took refuge in a little more textual research, and looked especially at the imagery the other characters use to describe the Jew Shylock: 'dog', 'cur', 'devil' . . . Often he and his people were equated with the devil. In one scene the same character draws the analogy twice.

Solanio and his crony Salerio (always referred to in theatrical shorthand as 'The Salads') are discussing the news that the merchant Antonio's ships have come to grief:

> SOLANIO . . .Why, the end is he hath lost a ship.
> SALERIO I would it might prove the end of his losses.
> SOLANIO Let me say 'amen' betimes, lest the devil cross my prayer, for here he comes in the likeness of a Jew.
> (*Enter Shylock.*)

And fifty lines later:

> SOLANIO Here comes another of the tribe; a third cannot be matched, unless the devil himself turn Jew.
> (*Enter Tubal.*)

Enter Tubal. One scene. Exit Tubal. The only other Jewish man in the whole of Shakespeare. Shylock's only ally. I had found my voice.

Apart from a peremptory mention by Jessica, Tubal is only referred to once elsewhere in the play. Shylock, when

discussing the fateful loan to Antonio, protests that he
cannot raise the whole sum immediately himself:

> What of that?
> Tubal, a wealthy Hebrew of my tribe,
> Will furnish me.

Rich and Jewish is all we know about Tubal. His appearance, his age, his marital status, his attitudes, aspirations,
hopes, fears, favourite colour, lucky number and taste in
music can only be speculated upon. A pristine blank page.

I started from the premise that Tubal would almost
certainly be unhappy with his brief, functional scene and
his virtual anonymity in the play. Just because he gives
him a mere eight short speeches in the play need not mean
that Shakespeare did not want Tubal sharing the stage
with his best friend at every opportunity. Why could he
not be present in *all* of Shylock's scenes, a silent witness?
An omnipresent Tubal could hear each of Shylock's utter-
ances, observe his relationships with other characters and
chart the narrative of the play. He could have moments of
solidarity, moments of dissent and, ultimately, moments
of compassion for his kinsman.

Unlike many major characters, Shylock is not greatly
given to soliloquy, and I found the solo speeches he does
have were remarkably easy to reassign as 'asides' to Tubal.
Shylock's references to Judaism are usually made in the
plural, as 'us' and 'our', and these were even more credible
as indicative of a companion on the stage. That Tubal's
presence is not acknowledged in the stage directions I
rationalised as merely bad editing. Shakespeare, after all,
was long dead and unable to protest his absence when the
First Folio was published.

Here was the chance for a minor character to step from the sidelines onto centre stage. And he would relish every moment of it. It was only a device, a conceit, but one I felt sure could be made to work. Frank agreed, and we took the play through several further drafts as the September deadline loomed.

Meanwhile, Jonathan in Salisbury had come up with an offer for me to direct Noël Coward's *Hay Fever* as the opening play of his autumn season and then to go straight into rehearsals for the Shylock project. What he was not able to offer was a budget which would allow me to pay Frank a realistic director's fee. The answer was obviously to offer Frank a part in *Hay Fever*. It would mean his working with me all day and then playing at night, but such a taxing regime held no fears for Frank, and it would make his remuneration a little less laughable.

Hay Fever is, for me, the best play in the Coward canon, a near-perfect comedy. In some other of his work, his extraordinary facility as a playwright often comes over as shallowness, and I'm not always sure whether it is Coward or his characters who are being patronising and snobbish. But in *Hay Fever* the results are so masterfully realised that I don't care.

I got together a wonderful cast of experienced and younger players, including Frank as David, the father of the appalling and hilarious Bliss family. Ostensibly the least theatrical member of that histrionic crew, David became in Frank's interpretation just as flamboyant and as funny as the rest of them. What we had both partly acknowledged as expedient casting turned out to be inspired. Polly Adams was a wonderfully endearing Judith Bliss, and she and Frank seemed to have as good a time onstage together as they gave our capacity audiences.

If all was mirth and merriment in the theatre from 7.30 on, our days were very earnest in comparison. We had less than a month to turn what was still a jumble of scenes, speeches, anecdotes and ideas into a full-length play. I would have gladly confessed to shallowness in exchange for just a little of Mr Coward's facility.

Posing as an Israelite

Frank is not a director. He is an actor who directs, which is a very different animal. There isn't a moment when he does not know what is going on in the performer's mind, and he constantly challenges you to do things differently, to do things better. He realised quite rightly that our preparation time was too short for reassurances and that what was needed was a creative ruthlessness. Together we assembled, dismantled and reassembled the play numerous times. Inevitably, my favourite bits were the first to go, they were less about enlightening the audience and more about my showing off. 'Kill your babies!' Frank urged, as he put a line through redundant passages in my script.

Together we solved what had seemed intractable problems. In the crucial duologue between Shylock and Tubal, Frank drilled me in the craft of playing both parts in a scene simultaneously. In the trial scene, he opened his box of tricks further and I found myself playing speeches of Shylock, Portia, Antonio and the Duke of Venice with barely a beat between impersonations. It was all founded on scrupulous technique, but he never let me lose sight of the emotional truth of each line. It was a rigorous process and, despite there being days when I wanted to resist jumping through Frank's hoops, a harmonious one. We were blessed with a stage manager, Siân Davies, whose retentive brain, attention to detail and obvious delight in our work made us into a dynamic trio.

Having solved the problem of who was to be the conduit of the play, there was still the decision as to how to

play Tubal. In *The Merchant*, I had played Shylock with a
slight middle-European accent, partly to distinguish him
from the non-Jewish characters in the play, but also because I had read that most Jewish moneylenders in Venice
would likely have been Ashkenazi Jews from Germany.
There is some justification for this in the text, where Shylock's sentence structure and occasionally eccentric vocabulary could mark him out as 'foreign'. We rationalised that
Tubal as 'a wealthy Hebrew of my tribe' should share
Shylock's vocal characteristics, even if his mere eight lines
in Shakespeare's play give little opportunity to display
them.

His lack of status in the dramatis personae was also an
opportunity to make his resentment comic. Comic relief
was a much-needed element given the grim nature of
much that I had written about anti-Semitism. Frank knew
exactly when and how to take the audience from the sombre
to the funny and vice-versa. He knew, too, how to exploit
their reaction without making them feel manipulated.

Tubal was emerging as an Everyman figure. He would
represent all small-part actors, all Shakespeare worshippers,
all Jews. The first two were easy for me. I had been a small-
part actor. I was a Shakespeare acolyte. But I was not a Jew.
There was a coyness in my script when I spoke of Jewish
history, Jewish practice or Jewish experience. I distanced
myself by talking of 'they' or 'them' not 'we' or 'us'. I feared
that for a lapsed Presbyterian to assume the awesome
mantle of Jewry might be an impertinence.

I spoke about this to Lara Bobroff, who was giving a
delightful performance as Sorrel, one of the impossible
twins, in *Hay Fever*. She told me about the Seder supper,
the highlight of the Passover Festival, which celebrates the
end of slavery in Egypt. When the story of that momen-
tous event is being retold as part of the celebration, the

Jews of history are always referred to as 'us' not 'them'. It makes the bond between the past and the present more tangible, it helps the celebrants to remember the potency of their collective lore. If I was playing a Jew, Lara said, I should have the courage of 'our' convictions.

Lara became my unpaid adviser on all matters Jewish. She helped me choose the right homburg hat from a store in Golder's Green. She taught me to sing the words in the Seder ritual – 'Why is this night different from all others?' – in Hebrew: 'Mah nishtanah halailah hazeh?' She explained that it is always the youngest member of the household who sings those words, so I added a shy toddler to my ever-expanding character list. It's important, she explained, for the child to understand as early as possible the meaning of Passover, the meaning of what it is to be born Jewish.

*

Of course, that was something I could never know. My father was a Presbyterian minister in Wales. My whole childhood and adolescence had been dominated by my status as the youngest son of the manse. Being a clergyman's child can give you ideas above your station. You live in a big house, with your own bedroom, sometimes your own study. The congregation treat you with a certain indulgence, a tolerance not always extended to the offspring of the laity. Additional status is bestowed by visiting clergy who always mention the incumbent, his wife and children, in their public prayers, often by name.

Even outside the chapel milieu, there is an aura attached to you. In my first primary school, I was spared a beating in the playground when some kid shouted out, 'You can't hit him, he's a . . . Christian!'

Wales, from which I am a happy and voluntary exile, has given me at least one attitude for which I am grateful. The Welsh, generally speaking, have no truck with feudalism. Wales has no aristocracy to speak of – they left for richer pastures when the Tudors came to power – so there is little of that knee-jerk respect for someone with a higher social standing that still permeates English society. When I grew up, deference, where it existed, was not to title or even money. It was primarily to heroes of the rugby field, but thereafter the most respected citizens were usually in teaching, medicine – and the church. That made me a little aristo. Lara told me that I had been the male goy equivalent of a Jewish Princess but without the shopping opportunities.

In reality, of course, our big house, owned by the church authorities, was freezing cold and pretty shabby. Secondhand clothes and the occasional ten-bob note from richer parishioners were never snubbed. My father's weekly income whilst I lived at home never even reached double figures, and the regime of our household was necessarily thrifty and, in retrospect, fairly strict.

My father was a devout, sincere and thoroughly honourable Christian. God always came first. Everything and everyone else, including my mother, had to make do with what was left of my father after his commitment to God. From his years as a penurious theology student and throughout the whole of his working life, his faith was absolute. There is no hierarchy in the Presbyterian Church of Wales, so no prospect or expectation of promotion or advancement. The sum total of my father's ambition was to serve his Maker. When he died, in his seventieth year, he knowingly approached death with a serenity and a certitude that was awe-inspiring.

His unshakeable faith and the pursuit of righteousness inevitably left casualties in its wake, most notably my mother, though I never heard her acknowledge it. She was expected to show the same single-minded devotion and sublimate everything else to being a clergyman's wife and helpmeet.

Their backgrounds were very different. My father was the son of a coal-miner in the Rhondda Valley. As the eldest child, he had been given the sole window of opportunity to escape that life and, after much family sacrifice, he won a scholarship to the university in Cardiff, where he resolutely pursued his calling for the church. In the Depression of the 1930s, austerity and sacrifice were quite simply taken for granted, and he never espoused any other way of life.

My mother was the last of eleven children born to well-off tradespeople in rural Cardiganshire. She was always very beautiful with jet-black hair and glorious blue eyes. She had been sent to a convent school in Belgium, spoke French, played the piano and had a fine contralto voice. She had travelled all over Europe, spent a year in South Africa and been wooed in chaste shipboard romances by several eligible bachelors. But it was my father she fell in love with. His first 'calling' was to her home town, where she first saw the skinny young minister riding around Llandovery on a bike, with a beret on his head like a French onion salesman. They married, and she spent the next forty years serving him and his God. She never persuaded him to part with the beret.

For a vivacious and attractive woman, the constrictions of chapel life must have sometimes been an agony: always having to keep the peace amongst the feuding old ladies who dominate all congregations, providing for every occasion the social skills that my shy father lacked, playing the piano at every sparse prayer meeting and Bible class. Like Caesar's wife, she had always to be above suspicion, or even a hint of rebellion. Her wardrobe and even the colour of her lipstick were restricted by propriety.

When my father was dying he said to her, 'Well, cariad, you'll be able to wear red again now.' A sincere, if belated, concession to a vibrant soul. But in truth, the purity of spirit that my father strove for all his life was quite effortlessly embodied in my mother. She fulfilled all her obligations with selflessness and joy and had enough loving energy left to be the most patient and sweet-natured mother to my older siblings, Alun and Bronwen, and to me. We each knew that in all our very different aspirations, we would always have her encouragement, approval and support. If my partiality puts that verdict in question, there are countless people spanning three generations who will attest to it. She is a woman entirely without envy, without greed and without spite. Now in her mid-nineties and no longer properly aware, she has somehow retained her sweetness and her capacity to give and inspire love.

There isn't a God, but if there were He would be as proud of her as I am. She also made the best chocolate cake in the history of baking.

*

My unbelief was not always so absolute. After church three times every Sunday, Christian Guild meetings, fellowship holidays, Sunday School exams and a social life that revolved around the chapel, faith was taken for granted. When I applied for university entrance, it was to read for a joint degree in Drama and Theology. With my background, I figured I might at least have a head start and, in reality, my barely adequate A Levels excluded me from any of the better-subscribed departments.

I should have realised my mistake on Day One. The Drama Department threw a welcome party in the converted gymnasium which served as a very atmospheric little theatre. It was all Rolling Stones and Strongbow cider and into the early hours with Otis Redding and sticky Spanish Sauternes. The Theology Department's welcome bash was a four o'clock tea party with a heady choice of Assam or Earl Grey and a collection of the dreariest students in Hull. In three weeks, after a half-hearted attempt to get to grips with New Testament Greek, I gave up on the God Squad and conned my way into the American Studies Department by lying about a passion for the history of the Civil War and the poetry of Edgar Allan Poe.

Apart from brief guest appearances at weddings and funerals, it was nearly thirty years before I again picked up a Bible that wasn't a prop and actually read it. But this time I was reading it not through the eyes of the youngest son of a preacher man but with the adopted eyes of a Jewish moneylender.

In his first scene, Shylock has a long, obscure and usually trimmed speech about Abraham, Jacob and Laban's grazing sheep. It comes during an exchange with Antonio, and the sequence demonstrates how both men are well acquainted with the Old Testament. And Shylock, when he turns down an invitation to dine with the merchant and his Christian friends on the grounds they might serve him pork, cites an episode from the New Testament:

> Yes, to smell pork, to eat of the habitation which your prophet, the Nazarite, conjured the devil into. I will buy with you, sell with you, talk with you, walk with you, and so following: but I will not eat with you, drink with you, nor pray with you.

Maybe he deliberately chooses not to mention Jesus, 'your prophet', by name, but if he was acquainted with His confrontation with the Gadarene swine he would certainly be acquainted with the manner of His death. It was, after all, the Gospels' assertion that the Jews were responsible for the execution of the Messiah that was largely to blame for the plight of Shylock and his people. St Matthew leads the way with a very accusatory finger. The time: AD 32. The place: Pontius Pilate's Palace, Jerusalem.

'Now at that feast the governor was wont to release unto the people a prisoner, whom they would.'

Significantly, there is no other record of this quaint custom of releasing a prisoner of the people's choice in any Roman or Jewish history book but as Antonio so quotably observes: 'The devil can cite scripture for his purpose.'

Here is the Gospel.

According to St Matthew, Chapter 27:

16: And they had then a notable prisoner called Barabbas.

17: Therefore when they were gathered together, Pilate said unto them, Whom will ye that I release unto you? Barabbas, or Jesus which is called Christ?

18. For he knew that for envy they had delivered him.

19: When he was set down on the judgement seat, his wife sent unto him, saying, Have thou nothing to do with that just man: for I have suffered many things this day in a dream because of him.

20: But the chief priests and elders persuaded the multitude that they should ask Barabbas, and destroy Jesus.

21: The governor answered and said unto them,
Whether of the twain will ye that I release unto you?
They said, Barabbas.

22: Pilate saith unto them, What shall I do then with
Jesus which is called Christ? They all say unto him, Let
him be crucified.

23: And the governor said, Why, what evil hath he
done? But they cried out the more, saying, Let him be
crucified.

24: When Pilate saw that he could prevail nothing,
but that rather a tumult was made, he took water, and
washed his hands before the multitude, saying, I am
innocent of the blood of this just person: see ye to it.

25: Then answered all the people, and said, His
blood be on us, and on our children.

26: Then released he Barabbas unto them: and when
he had scourged Jesus, he delivered him to be crucified.

'His blood be on us and on our children' has been the
primary excuse for two thousand years of Jewish persecution. It seems self-evident that the Gospels were propaganda intended to shift the blame from the all-powerful
Romans to the subject Israelites. Rome, of course, was the
prime target for Christian proselytising, and the Holy
Roman Empire the best testament to its success. By asserting that the Bible is the infallible word of God, the case
becomes unarguable.

Maybe if I had stuck it out in the Theology Department
all this would have been obvious to me long before I
revisited the Bible in my assumed persona. But I would
have been robbed of the chilling sensation which entered
my Shylock's heart on reading it again with Shylock's eyes.

*

With chunks from the Bible and plenty of Shakespeare, I knew that much of the play would be worth listening to. But I was less sanguine about the bits in between. It wasn't that I lacked faith in the material: my doubts were more about the play's structure or, rather, lack of it. The action darted about from Shakespeare's Globe to the Deutsches Theater in pre-war Berlin. One minute, the audience had to believe they were witnessing a twelfth-century massacre in York and the next, a matinée of *The Jew of Malta*. On good days, I thought we were creating a dynamic, kaleidoscopic piece of theatre. On bad days, I feared we had come up with a dog's dinner.

The key was obviously to reassure the audience that they were in safe hands. But in rehearsal I still felt stilted and unconvincing as Tubal, unable to find a rapport that was welcoming without being ingratiating. Maybe it was too predictable to start the play with a rational appeal for attention, and what was required was something more confrontational, more provocative. I tried opening with Shylock's blast for vengeance on Antonio in the trial scene:

> The pound of flesh which I demand of him
> Is dearly bought, is mine, and I will have it.
> If you deny me, fie upon your law!
> There is no force in the decrees of Venice.
> I stand for judgement. Answer, shall I have it?

It worked. After confronting such a vehement and uncompromising Shylock, I knew the audience would be relieved to meet Tubal, an approachable and dispassionate host. I got over the urge to try and tidy up the sequence of material, and felt free to take random excursions into history, theatrical lore, and the murky heritage of anti-Semitism. More confident in Tubal's persona, I felt the audience would follow me wherever I chose to take them.

With less than a week to go, Siân's prompt script, with all its cuttings, pastings and constant crossings out, was almost indecipherable. If I wasn't to be adrift in performance, it was time to put a stop to the rewriting, the additions and the subtractions and to consolidate the material.

Our budget had not stretched to a designer, so we had just used in rehearsal whatever props and furniture seemed appropriate at the time. The result was the visual equivalent of Siân's script: a jumble of boxes, books, coat racks, tables and chairs. Likewise, the costumes were a hotchpotch of rehearsal gear, cloaks and hats from the original *Merchant* production – plus a huge papier mâché nose and some pretty ludicrous wigs.

Our ruthless solution to this scenic chaos was to jettison nearly all of the furniture and to shove most of the small props, wigs, nose and hats into a large cabin trunk, which I could dive into from time to time. We borrowed a scene painter to stencil *Merchant of Venice* roughly across the front: necessity became the mother of a metaphor. I love and hate that trunk in equal measure. It has accompanied me faithfully around the world three-and-a-half times, and given me more grief at airport security than a box of grenades.

It can only happen once – the first performance of your first one-man show. And once is enough. It's a totally different terror from the first-night nerves you can share with the rest of the cast. Without them, the buck has only one place to stop. And you only have yourself to blame for being there in the first place.

We opened to a very partisan audience, mostly theatre staff and friends, who laughed and went quiet in all the right places. Straight after the show, Frank came backstage.

'That was fine. For a first performance. But I was sitting in the gallery, and you never looked at me once. You're up there all by yourself, the only other people you have to relate to are us, the audience. All of us. We are the other performer. If you ignore any of us, how are we expected to perform well?'

It was a lesson I could only learn in performance, and I have never forgotten it. Whether performing to a thousand people in some three-tiered culture palace in Eastern Europe or half-a-dozen folk in a converted chapel in south Yorkshire, I assume my audience are all potentially very good actors and it's my job to bring out the best in them.

Flying Solo

When Frank started touring *Macready* in the 1970s, he was following in the footsteps of a distinguished but not so numerous company of actors who had braved it alone. I never saw Gielgud's *Ages of Man* programme but as a schoolboy I had seen Emlyn Williams perform his solo Dickens programme at the Swansea YMCA. In his prime, he was a respected actor and very successful playwright, whose thriller *Night Must Fall* still crops up in the repertoire of regional theatres in need of a potboiler to help balance the books. Williams might have been almost forgotten now, but in recent years a theatre in his home town in North Wales has been named after him.

It was a little incongruous to see the great man on the same scruffy platform stage where we amateurs strutted and fretted in the local youth theatre. On the night of the performance, I was assigned to be his 'runner' and was astonished to see him, in the pokey area backstage that we had laboured to turn into his star's dressing room, tapping away on an ancient typewriter even as I announced curtain up. He stepped straight from the keyboard onto the stage, with no trace of the nerves I had assumed all players suffer.

His performance was as flawless as one might expect of a veteran who had been touring as Dickens for decades all over the world. All the vocal variety, all the vivid characterisations, all the melodrama and pathos were there. But the performance was strangely sterile. Brilliant technique, but no heart. I remember hoping that I would never quite cast off the churning feeling in the pit of the stomach that I associated with all live performing. I need not have worried: it is still there.

By the time I launched *Shylock*, solo performers were no longer a novelty, more of a plague. The generation of actors after mine were, whether they liked it or not, 'Thatcher's Children', which meant that, while making a living in the theatre had got more difficult, there was a whole new ethos of self-sufficiency abroad.

Most of my contemporaries took pride in not understanding the business or commercial aspects of the profession. We waited for the phone to ring, and if it didn't ring, we signed on the dole and/or got a day job. Nowadays, drama school graduates form limited companies before even getting their Equity cards. They form creative partnerships, take options on novels to make into movies, submit script breakdowns for drama series, sitcoms and corporate entertainments. Actor and entrepreneur are no longer mutually exclusive. And the one-man show is regarded as a compact, economical and marketable product.

Guy Masterson is an actor, writer, producer and entrepreneur who, as well as performing his own impressive one-man shows, also represents a formidable stable of other solo performers. After the first showing of *Shylock* in Salisbury, he asked me to join them, and I have him to thank for kick-starting my globetrotting. But the first few engagements under his management were, it has to be admitted, less than glamorous. With no track record, the show had to take whatever gigs were on offer, which turned out to be posh schools, because of the Shakespeare connection, and tiny rural arts centres, because I came cheap.

At Lancing, a leading boys' public school on the south coast, I played to a polite full house that seemed from my viewpoint to be almost entirely in profile. The girls from nearby Roedean had been invited over, and the staff had split the sexes up to right and left of the auditorium. The lure of the pheromones on either side proved more seductive to my teenage audience than whatever I was up to in front of them.

If the performances were too far out of London for me to return on the same evening, there was usually overnight accommodation stipulated in the contract. If the host organisation couldn't afford a hotel, I was billeted with local friends of the theatre. In one small Gloucestershire town, my hostess was a single, middle-aged woman called Sylvia who lived in a very grubby house with half-a-dozen cats. She was not unfriendly but there was something terribly earnest about her. Maybe it was her job?

'I work in a residential home for sexually abused boys,' she told me solemnly. 'It's very rewarding.' My bedroom was packed with tiny ceramic ornaments and stuffed toys. I had to move a whole menagerie of bunnies, pandas and koalas to get into my sagging bed, which was made up with brown Bri-Nylon sheets and candy-striped pillowslips that smelt of cigarettes and Brut.

Before Sylvia left for work next morning, she woke me at just after six o'clock with a cup of cat-smelling tea, and instructions to pull the front door to on my way out. 'And if you please,' she called from downstairs, 'be sure to make the bed up after you.' I certainly wasn't the first person to sleep in those sheets and I evidently wasn't going to be the last.

I decided after that, that there were things on tour up with which I would not put. So I should have turned and fled when, in response to my ringing the doorbell of a neat Victorian villa in Derbyshire, a very camp voice shrilled from inside, 'I hope you're okay with dogs, m'duck?' I *am* okay with dogs, but one at a time and only if they stay below crutch level. Here, four very assorted canines found something between my legs quite irresistible as I fought my way into Harold's kitchen. On the floor by the fridge was a fifth, much more docile, animal, so docile that I assumed it was asleep or possibly dead. Over a mug of dog-smelling tea, Harold wanted to know every detail of my personal life and was anxious that I should know every detail of his. Halfway through the narrative of why he and Roland had split up after all those years, he stopped suddenly, and took a deep sniff.

'Who's trumped?'

I took that to be the Derbyshire for 'farted'. It certainly wasn't me. He looked over at the prone creature by the fridge.

'Aaah, it's Dusty. She's shat herself. Again.' He took the sports page from the back of the *Derby Telegraph* and flapped over to the dog. Swooping down, he scooped up the single motion in a single motion.

'Y'know, there's people think that I should have her put down. But I say "How would you like to be put down just because you're a hundred and forty doggy years and got loose bowels?"'

With a flourish, he dropped the newspaper parcel into the bin and, coming straight back to the table, opened a circular tin and held up a biscuit.

'Fancy a Hobnob?'

On the pretext of having to go and re-park the car, I booked into the first hotel I came to and phoned Harold to explain that I had forgotten an urgent appointment next morning and was driving straight back to London.

'Well, who's a dizzy tart, then?' he called out over the noise of yapping.

Resolving no longer to accept the well-meaning hospitality of unsanitary animal lovers, I also decided that touring alone was too depressing. It's solitary enough onstage without also making the journeys, and setting up and dismantling the show by yourself. Then there's the lonesome post-performance pint or the candlelit dinner for one, with no one to tell you how well it had all gone in spite of there being only nine in the audience.

I managed to persuade a trio of actor friends, Andrew Branch, Phillip Joseph and Roger Llewellyn, to take it in turns to come with me and hold my hand when they had no work commitments of their own. We shared the driving, and organising of the lights and sound with the local technician and explored together the vibrant nightlife of towns like Chesterfield, Weymouth, Royal Tunbridge Wells, Mold and Preston. Preston beats Mold by a very short head for least scintillating town but wins hands down for the smallest audience: we played to six people, two of whom fell asleep the moment the lights dimmed and woke up just in time for the curtain call.

If the play was to have a life beyond the regional circuit, it needed proper exposure to national and international promoters. That meant the Edinburgh Fringe Festival.

*

'Twin!' Hilary King said to me (we were born within hours of each other, although I think on opposite sides of the planet), 'If you want the Fringe experience without leaving home, just stand under a cold shower ripping up fifty pound notes.'

Hilary and Roy, her affable bear of a husband, run their lively 'Red Pear' theatre company from the most seductive small-scale venue on the global circuit: a bijou theatre in the very heart of Antibes, on the southern French coast.

That they forsake it every summer for the mayhem of the Festival just demonstrates how unavoidable Edinburgh is.

To break even there is a huge achievement; to make money is almost unheard of. You do it for the experience or for the connections you make for life back in the real world. To relish the ordeal, you really have to be very young, very energetic, and very resilient. You need to be able to function without sleep, largely under the influence of drink or drugs, to hold conversations at screaming level in bars you'd never be seen dead in outside a Scottish August, to sit through execrable offerings from fellow participants and to take no offence at being totally ignored by press, audience and more successful performers.

Guy Masterson has a thick-enough skin and sufficient nous to have mastered the beast and to emerge each year with a clutch of awards and his liver and hearing more or less intact. In 1998 *Shylock* was one of several shows he booked into the prestigious Assembly Rooms complex on elegant George Street for a whole, cold, wet month.

The sound of four hands clapping is very lonely noise. At the second show, we had doubled that, and two of the eight belonged to Arnold Wesker. Having a world-class dramatist making up a quarter of your audience is nerve-wracking enough but when he has also written a play called *Shylock*, the stakes are even higher.

Arnold Wesker hates *The Merchant of Venice*. He thinks it is an incitement to racial hatred and should never be performed. His response in the mid-1970s was to write a remarkable play called *The Merchant* (subsequently re-named *Shylock*), in which Shylock and Antonio are the best of friends and the flesh bond between them is a joke that turns sour under the inflexibility and innate anti-Semitism of Venetian law. The play premiered at Birmingham

Rep, had various rehearsed readings in London and would have played a season on Broadway if its star, the great Zero Mostel, had not died before the official opening.

Arnold is perplexed and angered at the play's lack of mainstream recognition in Britain. It has forced him to conclude, erroneously in my opinion, that the British theatre establishment is, like the laws of Venice, anti-Semitic. I had had first-hand experience of his play when performing *The Merchant of Venice* at Salisbury. Jonathan Church had written to Arnold asking if we might stage a reading of his *Shylock*. One of the most generous of men, Arnold gave his permission freely, but couldn't resist the suggestion that we should perform a three-week run of his play and do a rehearsed reading of *The Merchant of Venice* instead.

He was characteristically generous about my play too, and although I wouldn't claim to have lessened his antipathy towards Shakespeare's original, I think he found mine a valid contribution to the debate and was at pains to promote it wherever he could.

But the only things to ensure good audiences at Edinburgh are a cutting-edge comedian, full-frontal nudity, an outrageous title or a five-star review in *The Scotsman*. Excluded from every other category, I was hugely relieved to qualify for the last. Owen Dudley Edwards, the doyen of Festival critics, greeted *Shylock* with something approaching rapture, declared it 'The Main Event' and referred to it in later jottings as a 'masterpiece'. All the other Edinburgh press concurred and when the Sunday papers came out, I got my first-ever, unqualified rave review in a national newspaper: 'Armstrong is nothing short of incredible . . . This is an exceptional piece of theatre . . . everyone should see it.' (*Independent on Sunday*)

I wasn't used to this. On the first Monday of the run, I was huddling behind a curtain at the side of the stage, waiting for the house to trickle in as usual and heard instead an usher announce: 'Would the queue for *Shylock returns* please form a line up the main staircase!' We were a total sell-out. Admittedly the venue sat fewer than two hundred people but when you are competing with shows entitled *Fucking Our Fathers* (sic) and *Wiping My Mother's Arse* (sic-ker), any sort of full house is a miracle.

I had just had my fiftieth birthday and was suffering all the irrational traumas that come with that unwelcome milestone. What happened to me in Edinburgh didn't make me rich, or a household name, or even more employable, but it did give me the sort of professional fulfilment for which I had been striving for over thirty years. It was a small thing, but mine own, and if Steve had been alive to share the novelty of my success, I think I might have burst.

Swans and Kiwis

My first booking after Edinburgh was a dream date. I played two performances at the Swan Theatre in Stratford-upon-Avon. The Swan was built with money from a rich American donor long after my undistinguished season with the RSC, but as a mere audience member, I had always found it the most satisfying and exciting of theatre spaces. The stage projects into an intimate auditorium with the audience on three levels, giving the same rare proximity that can still be found in the few surviving music-hall houses. The impression that you can almost touch everyone in the audience is a particular gift to the solo performer. Through both performances I was fighting a combination of Edinburgh fatigue and a very nasty flu bug, but nothing would have kept me off that stage.

A few weeks later, I played Stratford again. To get to the theatre, we drove down Prospero Place, bypassing Hamlet Street, Tybalt Street and Avon Street, and stopped briefly under the clock tower where three times a day Romeo and Juliet emerge from various orifices in the mock-Tudor structure to give a five-minute performance, glockenspiel-style.

The venue, a converted cinema built at the end of the Great War, had a platform stage perched high above an auditorium with plush red seats that still retained their original ashtrays. We had brought our own very basic lighting and sound equipment. The Swan it was not.

Our host was the mayor of Stratford and the audience was the citizens of Stratford: Stratford, California; Stratford,

Connecticut; Stratford, Ontario; Stratford, Texas and even a few from Stratford, England.

Here we all were in Stratford-upon-Patea, New Zealand, within reach of the great Mount Taranaki, a snowcapped dormant volcano with stunning views of the countryside all around. The occasion was a big jamboree to celebrate something. Probably that they all came from Stratford. It turned out to be quite a party. At one point, I started taking bookings to perform in all the Stratfords in rotation, but I can't remember in what order, and neither, I suspect, could my hosts.

Thanks to Guy Masterson, New Zealand was my first overseas booking with *Shylock*, and my first trip downunder. I have Kiwi friends in England who are always telling me how thrilled they are to have escaped from the dreary place with its Scottish Presbyterian attitudes, ghastly food and cultural sterility. I obviously went to the other New Zealand. From the tropical paradise of the Bay of Islands in the North Island to the eerie majesty of Milford Sound in the South Island, New Zealand manages to live up to all the tourist-brochure hype, and then some. And in a country where nothing much is supposed to happen, I even managed to cause a police alert.

Close to Queenstown, the tourist capital of the South Island, is a tiny settlement called Arrowtown, founded during the New Zealand gold rush. It's a heritage site, and its one main street looks very like a similar-sized settlement in the American West, except that instead of saloons and hardware stores, it is lined with tasteful souvenir and tea shops as if the gold rush had happened somewhere in the Cotswolds.

I had come to perform in the War Memorial Hall, a glorified Scout hut with that unmistakable and reassuring smell of the tea urn and sour milk. After a morning setting up the equipment, we had a late lunch, still giving me time to take a nap before the show. Amidst the boxes of bunting and broken wicker chairs in the back room, I cleared a space on a wooden crate beneath the window that looked onto the pavement, and pulling Shylock's old black coat up around my shoulders and his homburg hat over my face, I fell asleep.

Within an hour I was being shaken awake by an armed policewoman and asked for some identification. A local resident had reported that a derelict had broken into the beloved Memorial Hall and was sleeping it off in the back. The policewoman had driven a full twenty minutes from Queenstown to investigate, Arrowtown having no police presence of its own. With such vigilant residents, it obviously doesn't need one.

The only place in New Zealand that I was less than enchanted by was Napier, in the otherwise glorious Hawke's Bay area. An earthquake in 1931 more or less levelled the original town and, because of such unlucky timing, the phoenix which replaced it was almost entirely art deco in style. Now, a bit of art deco is alright in its place but an entire city is like an endless diet of iced fondant fancies. And the populace are mighty proud of their status as art deco capital of the world. It gives them a very un-New Zealand-like smugness, which leaves a taste in the mouth not dissimilar to that left by iced fondant fancies.

After two months in the country, I started making half-genuine enquiries about immigration. Of course, I was too long in the tooth, didn't have the right job, or enough money to qualify, but I could see myself growing old in a young country of staggering beauty amongst delightful people, working in a very vibrant arts scene with a quality of life way beyond my means back in Blighty. For the seafood and Sauvignon blanc alone, it would be worth trading passports. But would I have been driven mad and forced to seek asylum back in west London because of that accent?

The month I spent in the capital city, Wellington, was one of the happiest of my life. Wellington is built on steep hills around a beautiful coastline, and bears more than a passing resemblance to San Francisco, but without the obesity, rapacious greed and disproportionate number of crazy people in that once life-enhancing city.

One of the first people I met in Wellington had come out over thirty years before on the ten-pound boat ticket which was the inducement to get people to move to Australasia when those countries were desperate for settlers. In those days, they might even have taken a middle-aged thespian without a pension. Ray Henwood is now a handsome, silver-haired man in his sixties, running a new and innovative theatre called Circa, just yards from the lapping ocean. He had no memory of me at all, even when I prompted him with reminiscences of my first-ever stage appearance, in *Murder in the Cathedral*. But then why would the glamorous, rugby-capped star of countless school plays, who had returned to his alma mater as a junior chemistry teacher, remember a chubby, twelve-year-old schoolboy playing one of the chorus of Canterbury women wearing his sister's bra stuffed with lavatory paper?

Ray and his wife Caroline, a very high-spirited High Court Judge, were a wonderful advertisement for their adopted country, and all the people I met were welcoming, co-operative and open-minded. But I wanted to find out if their friendliness and tolerance were universal, I wanted to know if the theme of anti-Semitism in my play would have any local resonance here. The problem was I couldn't find any Jews to ask. I never met a single Jewish person the whole time I spent in the country. In New

Zealand they are a very rare breed. The 1997 census, from a population of just over three-and-a-half million, identified just 4,809 Jews. By comparison, there is a huge majority of Christians, including over forty thousand Mormons, and there are six times as many Hindus and over three times as many Muslims as there are Jews. I wish I could fathom out why, because in my experience most Jews know a good thing when they see it.

Macbeth and Mickey Mouse

On my way back from New Zealand, I broke my journey in San Francisco, but I didn't go just to make invidious comparisons. I was there to give a concert performance of *Shylock* for the annual conference of the Shakespeare Association of America. It's a big bash for university faculty, who leave their ivory towers all over the States and descend on a major city for a long weekend of lectures, papers, symposiums, and even, I am told, some serious partying.

The Shakespeare industry in America can be quite alarming. Academics are just desperate to find something, anything, to say about a play that may not have been said before, publish it and secure their careers. Their conclusions range from the intriguing to the seriously deranged, and Shakespeare would have probably found them all hilarious, especially the sizeable minority who disapprove of the plays being performed at all, claiming that performance sullies the purity of the text.

I'd had experience of the best and the worst of them working for a company started by one of the sanest and most performer-friendly of Shakespeare professors, Homer Swander of Santa Barbara, California. Back in the 1970s, he had asked Patrick Stewart, long before the stardom of *Star Trek*, to talk to some American students he'd brought over to Stratford. Stewart protested that he wouldn't know what to say; he was an actor, not a teacher. But in exchange for a bottle of good Scotch, he did his best and both he and the students found it a revelation.

That spawned a part-time company made up of ex and current members of the RSC who tour campuses bi-annually, performing and teaching Shakespeare. Over the years, a pattern of work has emerged which makes it unique and uniquely exciting to be part of. The company's credo is almost ascetic: five actors, never more, take a Shakespeare text, divide the roles between them and perform it in its entirety. There is no director, no designer, and virtually no budget. Instead, there is a fierce democracy of players who, probably for the first time in their careers, are severally and jointly responsible for everything that their young audiences will see.

It's not an easy process. It requires a tricky combination of assertiveness and humility, as well as a rigorous discipline. But at the end of a tour there is a huge sense of achievement too. Not just of having made the play work, but of having gone into dozens of classrooms over the weeks with the mission to convince American undergraduates that Shakespeare is not dull, not deadly. Sometimes, of course, you fail – like the time I was trying to convince nineteen-year-olds in Philadelphia to empathise with Antony and Cleopatra's passion.

'Hey, this is gross! These old guys, still . . . doing it!'

'They're not old,' I insisted. 'They're in their forties. My age!'

'Yeeeh! Gross.'

One young group even had trouble finding the romance in *Romeo and Juliet:* it turned out their professor had told them the play was really about necrophilia.

By the end of eight or ten weeks on the road, playing and teaching on a different campus each week, virtually all the relationships in the troupe come under strain. Moody silences have turned into furious rows, fists have been raised, decades-old friendships have crumbled, and actors have even delayed their return flights home to avoid being on the same plane as a now-hated colleague.

On my first tour, I nearly killed my old friend, John Fraser. Not because of an artistic difference, but because of a ten-ton truck. I had volunteered to drive us both to our classes at the college in a sleepy Texan town called Nagadoches. On the way back, I simply turned into the road and looked the wrong way . . . I have never driven in the States since.

John was a film star in the 1960s. He was one of the leads in *El Cid*, Bosie in *The Trials of Oscar Wilde*, and played opposite Catherine Deneuve in Polanski's *Repulsion*. He has great stories to tell about that period, but it's evident that his greatest satisfaction came from years of touring with The London Shakespeare Group and, before that, as half of one of Auntie Val's early Shakespeare Duos. He wrote a wonderfully atmospheric book about that experience, called *The Bard in the Bush*. It is no longer in print, alas, but one of the American professors we encountered, who was probably writing a paper on how Shakespeare was really an Ashanti chief, was anxious to read it. Clarice was a determined woman in her early sixties with her iron-grey hair swept severely back into a bun. She dressed in sensible shoes and tweeds, even in blazing heat, as though she was impersonating an English Shakespeare scholar from the 1950s.

She whisked us off to the university library and introduced us to the magic of the internet. It was the nineties and neither John nor I had discovered cyberspace. She was absolutely certain she could find the book and she duly typed the details into the 'search'.

Title: '*The Bard in the Bush*'
Author: 'John Fraser'
Publisher: 'Granada'

There was a few seconds' pause before we got the results. We were informed that there were no exact matches. The nearest was: *A Hand in the Bush – The Fine Art of Vaginal Fisting* by Deborah Addington. It got a five-star reader rating and was reduced by twenty per cent. There was even a 'second-hand' copy on offer for five bucks . . . Clarice said not a word, and John and I had self-inflicted stigmata on our palms for days afterwards from the effort to behave ourselves.

As well as the performing and teaching, our five-handed troupe was often asked for short one-person pieces on a Shakespearean theme. I put together a sort of illustrated lecture comparing Macbeth and Richard III and called it *Hand in Hand to Hell*, a quote from Richard's battle speech at the end of the play. Fifty-odd minutes of showing off, it was a mixture of soliloquies from both plays, bits of theatre history and a few anecdotes.

In Orlando, Florida, we were asked to spend a weekend working at the newly opened Disney Institute: 'An educational facility at Disney World, allowing vacationers to learn while they play.' This move upmarket offered families an alternative to Cinderella's castle or a simulated voyage to the bottom of the ocean, and gave Disney a chance to charge them through the nose for a more creative and cerebral experience.

The campus is built on acres of manicured and lushly green lawns, intersected by man-made streams and quaint Japanese-style bridges. The complex hotel is built in colonial style and painted in reassuring pastel shades. With transport provided by motorised buggies and with the staff wearing permanent beaming smiles, the whole enterprise is eerily reminiscent of the 1960s cult TV series, *The Prisoner.*

The Institute's prospectus offered courses from cookery to creative writing and from music-making to macramé.

Our weekend was called 'Playing with Shakespeare'. As well as conducting workshops with youngsters getting overexcited about the contents of the witches' cauldron in *Macbeth* ('eye of newt, and toe of frog, wool of bat and tongue of dog'), I was asked to present *Hand in Hand to Hell.*

Their brand new multi-purpose theatre had a super-advanced lighting system, state-of-the-art acoustic enhancement, totally silent air conditioning, armchair seats and all the atmosphere of a crematorium chapel. But my audience was eager and attentive. Especially attentive was a sharp-suited man in his forties who sat in the middle of the front row, a notepad on his knee, nodding sagely from time to time.

I came to the speech where Macbeth debates with himself about whether or not he should commit the murder of King Duncan. He weighs up the pros and cons, the prospects and the perils. It is a complex, and beautifully constructed soliloquy, which I went on to describe as 'a ride through Macbeth's conscience.' The man in the front row rapidly scribbled something down, and I was aware from thereon that he was paying less attention to me than to his notebook.

At the end of the presentation, he approached with the hallmark Disney handshake, firm and manly with strong eye contact. 'Mr Armstrong, will you visit with us at the Imagineering Centre? I am going to ask my imagineers to construct a model based upon your idea of "a ride through Macbeth's conscience".' He opened the notebook. 'The ride will start here,' he pointed to a rough sketch complete with stick figures, 'with three witches upon a heath . . . thunder, lightning. Next, the Macbeth's castle . . . remote and fog-bound. The King's bedchamber . . . screams and confusion. A lavish coronation. The slaying of Banquo . . .'

You can take the good old boy out of Disney, I thought, but you can't take Disney out of the good old boy.

*

For *Hand in Hand to Hell*, I had started by using a lectern, but with the confidence of repeated outings, I dispensed with it and ended up with something approaching a rudimentary one-man show. Now back in the States with *Shylock*, I was hoping to get back onto the lucrative university circuit and the Shakespeare Association seemed like a good place to showcase it. If nothing else, it would split the marathon journey from New Zealand to London into two segments.

I had been given the number of an American producer based in San Francisco who might be persuaded to come and see the show. It seemed such a long shot that I nearly didn't bother, but when I got through to his office, we at least found we had something in common. Jet lag. Robert Friedman had just got off the plane from Venice and was feeling as disoriented as I was. We both doubted that he would be in any state to come the following morning to see an actor in a different time zone performing a play set in the city he had recently left, in a lecture hall in the basement of the Hyatt Hotel. But he wished me luck.

In the audience of professors and would-be professors next day there was one person chuckling in a very unacademic manner. He came up to me afterwards: 'I'm taking you to the best restaurant in San Francisco.' Exaggeration, I was to find, is one of Robert's most endearing qualities. I found, too, that I had got myself, almost by accident, an American producer.

Getting in a State

Robert is either six months younger or six months older than me, I can never remember which. We could be brothers except I look a bit more Jewish than he does. We both sleep badly but, unlike me, he refuses to resort to alcohol and prescription drugs and so is consequently almost always sleep-deprived. He knows, or wants to know, everybody he meets and assumes that everybody returns the compliment. This is not always the case. His genuine overtures of friendship sometimes meet with a mild rebuff or an indifference which he simply does not comprehend. This is less naivety than a genuine belief in the sociability of humankind, so to watch his crest fall at the natural aloofness of a Londoner or the native rudeness of a Parisian is really rather touching.

This optimism extends to his work, where his faith and enthusiasm for the arts is only occasionally diminished by the realities of an increasingly philistine world. They say you can know more about a person from the company they keep or the books they read, but in Robert's case, a list of the artists he represents would be even more revealing. It's an eclectic, almost eccentric stable of mostly musicians: a solo lutenist, pianist, and guitar player, ensembles for early music, sacred music, and jazz. He loves nearly all music with a totally unpretentious zeal. He represents a Russian ballet troupe, a Canadian jazz ballet company, and a musical revue on Shakespeare. He has two actors who do one-man shows, one who does Macbeth in the manner of *The Simpsons*, and me. According to Robert, we are all 'the best', and he really believes it.

It's Robert's faith in *Shylock* that now takes me to the States a couple of times each year to do a mixed-bag circuit of theatres, colleges and Jewish community centres. I've been to places in America that even Americans haven't heard of, and performed in most major cities. I've played to audiences whose response has varied from the ecstatic to the comatose. We've been sold out, and we've cancelled shows from lack of interest.

The first tour that Robert set up for me he admitted was a trial run, but neither of us could have known how much of a trial it would turn out to be. For a start, we had underestimated the problems of getting me a visa to perform in the States. American Equity, the actors' union, are very jealous of their members' rights and determined not to let the small amount of work available to stage actors be taken from them by visiting foreigners. If you're a star, there is less of a problem, but in my case they were very unwilling to grant me entry.

Eventually, by soliciting a strange variety of worthies, from a right-wing US senator to a liberal Californian rabbi, and by getting a letter from the radio actors' union conceding that I was, at least, a 'star' of radio – thank you, *Archers*! – I got my authorisation. Visas come in dozens of different types and mine was about the least impressive you can get, listing me as an 'ethnic' artist. This may refer to my impersonating a Jew or maybe even my being a Welshman, but I didn't care and would have laid claim to being a Zambian fan dancer just to get in.

I was due to fly to Dallas on a Monday with my first performance on the Wednesday afternoon, but by the preceding weekend there was no sign of my authorisation from the States. Monday was a Bank Holiday. If you like days off, working in an embassy must be the ideal job because you get to celebrate all the host country's national holidays as well as your own. There was no way I was going to get my passport stamped in time for the flight.

It did cross my mind to just go and pose as a tourist, hoping they wouldn't open my trunk and quiz me about the curious wigs, hats and replica Jew badges I travel with: 'Oh, I just love to dress up . . . especially on Yom Kippur!' But then I remembered a cautionary tale from Frank Barrie, who had, coincidentally, flown into the very same Dallas airport the previous year with a tourist visa and been honest enough to tell the immigration officer that he would, in fact, be giving a couple of Shakespeare lecture performances.

'Not with this visa you ain't!'

Frank had been refused entry, not even allowed to make contact with his hosts waiting the other side of the baggage claim, put back on the very same plane and deported. As well as the cancellation of his engagement, the personal humiliation *and* the black mark on his immigration status, he had flown for twenty hours out of twenty-four and hadn't even had time to get his duty-frees. I wasn't going to risk it.

The authorisation came through on Tuesday afternoon, I was on a flight next morning, driven from Dallas airport to the venue, and performing a matinée within three hours of touchdown. That may conjure up a vision of my bursting through the stage door, a quick exchange of pleasantries with the ancient but irreplaceable stage-door man, scooping up my first night tributes, bonding briefly with my sweet and unflappable dresser, eager and efficient technical staff racing through my sound and light plots just in time for me to walk into my spotlight, breathless but empowered by the magic of theatre. I wish.

Robert had contracted me for three weeks to North-wood University. Northwood University is what is called a 'business' university. A private institution, it prepares its young students for a life at the cutting edge of commerce. 'Come here . . . and you'll develop your own business plan for life,' it claims, and the university offers degrees only in Business and Management. As well as the usual subjects like Accountancy and Law, you can study Fire Science Management, Automotive Marketing and even Automotive After-marketing.

To fulfil the terms of their charter, Northwood has to make some provision for the arts: 'The Arts make great Business Partners' is another of their credos. Sam, my host, was in charge of their arts programme and every year he brought an artist to tour Northwood's three campuses in Texas, Florida and Michigan. They had had a sculptor, a Russian mime, a harpist, and this particular year they had me.

The matinée performance of *Shylock*, for which I had been so eager to cross the Atlantic, played to about thirty sullen youths and a handful of listless girls in a lecture hall with no stage lighting and a portable CD player through which my soundtrack sounded as if it was playing under-water. Unenthusiastic would be a polite way to describe the audience response, and after the show, I was feeling not a little despondent as I left the stage.

An unsmiling girl approached me and thrust a piece of lined paper at me.

'Will you please sign this, sir?'

Behind her I saw a line forming, each student holding a similar blank piece of paper. How quick I had been to dismiss their reticence as indifference. Theatregoing was evidently a new experience for them, which explained their lack of reaction, but they somehow knew it was a special event, even in such unpromising circumstances, and wanted to acknowledge that. I took her pen.

'What's your name?' I asked her.

'Marcia.'

I wrote, 'To Marcia, with all best wishes . . . '

'Hell, no!' She took the paper from my hand and turned it over. 'Just put your name. We've got to have your name at the end of the class to prove we sat through it . . . all of it. We miss a credit if we don't have your name. Here.'

As well as the performances, I was contracted to take classes on 'Shakespeare and the Drama'. I find teaching infinitely harder than performing and much more nerve-wracking. It didn't take me long to realise that my usual approach about the universality of Shakespeare's art, the potency of his language and the indispensable role of the theatre in a civilised society would be as appealing to these students as a lecture on Automotive Aftermarketing would be to me.

It was a humbling revelation, not anything to be proud of. After all, automotive aftermarketing is probably what makes the world go round. I would learn from it. I would meet them on their own ground. I sat up late one night preparing a class on 'Shakespeare the Businessman'. How easy would it be to see the world through their eyes?

Son of a tanner or glove merchant, an actor who some-how raised £100 ($150 to you) to buy a holding in Richard Burbage's Globe Theatre Company. A sharer in the box-office receipts. A craftsman who targeted his work to please all his audience (his customers) in order to maximise his income. How was I doing? Company. Share. Customers. Income.

And what about *The Merchant of Venice*? A play with money at its heart. Without finance, Bassanio cannot go in pursuit of his rich and lovely bride. Lending money at interest, usury in Shakespeare's time, was forbidden to Christians according to Biblical teaching, but Shakespeare's own father had been accused of it. After all, isn't usury only another word for banking? What did Shakespeare really feel about moneylenders and their profession?

It would hardly put me in line for a professorship, but there were surely enough themes and questions there to make for a lively interaction, so I wasn't entirely fearful when the time for the class came round.

Americans start their university careers earlier than their British counterparts and their classrooms still tend to resemble schoolrooms. The students sit at, or rather in, a curiously old-fashioned contraption which is both seat and writing desk. Given the dimensions of the average American undergraduate, it is a singularly inappropriate piece of furniture, and they tend to look awkward and uncomfortable squeezed into, or hanging out of, their desks. But on this occasion, I could see that their primary purpose is to wedge the student in a position which will prevent them slipping onto the floor when ennui or even sleep overcome them. Within twenty minutes of my starting, I could see the soles of more pairs of trainers than I could see faces. The eyes that were still open and focused looked at me with something like contempt or maybe it was just incomprehension. I panicked, wound up my presentation and asked for questions. There was a very long silence. Then a girl at the back of the room must have taken pity on me. Forcing herself out of whatever reverie my lecture had induced, she asked chirpily, 'Hey, why did you call your play *Skylark*?'

I did find one ally at the Dallas campus, an English Language teacher with an infectious passion for nineteenth-century American poetry. He introduced me to some writers I had never heard of and gave me a splendid limited-edition copy of Horace Traubel's *With Walt Whitman in Camden* as a gift.

One night, he took me out with a favourite pupil, a shy jock called Billy, to show me the route that the Kennedy motorcade had taken on the day of his assassination. We stood on the grassy knoll, looked up at the Depository window, speculated about the 'magic bullet', and ended up in a sports bar.

'Now, Billy here is learning to appreciate the beauties of poetry, aren't you, Billy?' he drawled. With his slow, gentle southern accent he might have been a character from a play that Tennessee Williams almost wrote. Billy took a long swig from his bottle of Bud. 'I was telling him only the other day, wasn't I, Billy, about the meeting of our great Walt Whitman with your great Oscar Wilde.' He turned back to Billy. 'Now, Billy, those two men were different in so many ways, but they also had something in common ... ' Billy shifted uneasily on his bar stool.

In my second week, I noted big changes in the move from Northwood's campus in Dallas, Texas, to their base in Palm Beach, Florida. The weather was warmer, the pace of life gentler, the per capita income even greater. The students, alas, were identical.

To escape the campus, I befriended the college arts co-ordinator, Sally. She looked no older than the students, had spiky green hair and lots of piercings, smoked, swore and hated Republicans. She felt no more at home at Northwood than I did, and I never fathomed why she wanted or how she got the job in the first place. Bribing her with dinner and a trip to the theatre, I persuaded her to drive me into town. It was a curious journey, where every other vehicle seemed to be an enormous old Cadillac purring along at fifteen miles an hour with, apparently, nobody behind the wheel.

'Snowbirds,' she offered. 'They fly down from Michigan or Ohio or some godawful shithole to winter in Florida. They like to drive their own cars so they get them trucked here. They're all about a hundred and twenty, four foot and a fart high, mostly widows and stinking rich. They'd get there quicker with a walking frame!' She overtook a huge pink Cadillac straight out of a Doris Day movie. 'If you look now you'll see a pair of little gnarled hands gripping onto the steering wheel.' As we passed there was a brief flash of light, like a laser, from where the driver should have been. 'See? Jeez, the size of those rocks!'

At the theatre the entire audience were, with no exaggeration, in their eighties or older. And so were the ushers. Just before the show began there was a recorded announcement:

'Ladies and gentlemen, welcome to tonight's performance. In the very unlikely event of an emergency, please make your way to the exits located at the front and rear of the auditorium. For those of you unable to make your own way to the exits, the ushers will be happy to assist you, so ...'

' ... then you're really fucked!' Sally breathed in my ear.

Midland, Michigan, was the third and final Northwood campus on my itinerary, and my last chance to redeem myself. I abandoned the disingenuous attempt to portray Shakespeare as a canny operator who also wrote plays, and tried to engage them in the narrative of *The Merchant*.

For those for whom a missed credit was a small price to pay for not having to sit through my show, the story came as a surprise. I sensed that I had at last got their attention. There was even a mild frisson when I revealed the terms of Shylock's bond, a whispered chorus of 'That is ... gross!' I warmed to the theme:

'Haven't all of you, at one time, longed for your own "pound of flesh"?'

A great lout in the front row, who looked as if he'd need a surgical procedure to get him out of his toddler's chair, slid his fingers from the desk top down between his fat thighs and squeezed his crutch. 'All the time,' he groaned, just loud enough to be heard by the whole class. At that moment they remembered that they weren't there to be impressed by me, and I remembered that I was wasting my time.

Two Exits to Thunderous Silence

Robert had broken a promise he'd made to himself years before: not to put on a show using his own money. He had decided to produce *Shylock* in his home town of San Francisco and, not finding himself fighting off would-be sponsors, he was underwriting the project himself.

'It'll be okay when we get the man standing on the chair,' he had said. The first time he said it I assumed it was an American theatrical expression not familiar to me. 'Break a leg!' is, after all, a total and inexplicable American import, and there are plenty of differences in the jargon we use either side of the pond. We say 'Interval'; they say 'Intermission'. We refer to the final call before curtain up as 'Beginners please!'; they say 'Places please!' We call the front curtain, 'the tabs'; they reasonably enough call it the 'front curtain'. And in Britain, all curtains used to mask the stage or create a neutral space are called 'blacks', because they always are. This is not so in America. When a stage manager for one of our five-handed tours was sending technical specifications to a theatre in Tennessee and sent them a fax which read, 'Please ensure before our arrival that all blacks are hung at the back of the stage', there was a swift and perplexed response.

As we booked me into a very seedy hotel in downtown San Francisco for the month of the engagement, Robert, seeing my face fall, said, 'You'll be out of here and in the Hyatt . . . when we get the man standing on the chair .'

The man standing on the chair turned out to be the symbol adopted by the *San Francisco Chronicle* atop of a

rave review. The *Chronicle* was the only paper with clout,
it seemed. According to Robert, the man standing on the
chair guaranteed full houses, a profit for him and the
Hyatt for me.

Like the star rating now, alas, used in many English
newspapers, it was graded, but instead of one to five stars,
it was a series of five little cartoons. First, the man standing on the chair, clapping. A smash hit! Second, the man
sitting on his chair but clapping enthusiastically. A success! Third, the man just sitting on the chair. Good, but not
outstanding. Fourth, the man asleep in the chair. A flop.
Fifth, an empty chair. A disaster!

So convinced was Robert that we'd get the man
standing on the chair that he had booked us into a
capacious and unsuitable venue miles from the centre of
town, named after Ira Gershwin and his wife. Even before
we opened I thought it would bode better if they'd named
it after George.

In the event, we got the man sitting in the chair, sans
clapping. Good, but not great. Robert's touching confidence that the wretched little sod would be on his feet
meant that he had taken out virtually no publicity, either
on TV or in the papers. The bookings were lousy. We cancelled several performances and I stayed put in my seedy
hotel. I don't think it was the kind of establishment where
the proprietors keep abreast of artistic events in their city,
so at least they didn't ask for the whole month's room
rental in advance.

Robert, supportive and solicitous throughout, was
understandably worried about his investment and I was
dejected, angry with myself for not having given a better
performance on the opening night to get that stupid acco-
lade. Irrationally, I began to hate San Francisco. But my
disillusion with what I had always regarded as the most

lively and liberal city in the States was not just to do with my personal failure. Personal failure was everywhere.

This was the height of the dot-com boom where the successful had become absurdly and obscenely wealthy. It threw into even greater relief the plight of the ones who hadn't made it. Coming out of my hotel, each day I was accosted by beggars on every street corner. This was nothing new, as the city, unlike New York, had always had a relaxed attitude towards its indigent citizens. The culture has so changed in New York that, on a recent visit, the dollar bill I graciously volunteered to a bag lady, covered entirely in clear plastic on a freezing February night, was met with a furious and chastening cry: 'Where do you *get* your presumption!'

But on past visits to San Francisco the panhandlers had seemed relaxed, simply high or drunk or maybe a little nuts. Now they were desperate and often aggressive. Most alarmingly, they didn't look like good casting, they looked like me or my friends or most of the other people walking the city streets. They looked like ordinary people who had had just a little too much bad luck, lost their jobs, had a breakdown, taken a trip too many or a glass too much. For them, the little man had just fallen off his wretched chair, with no net to catch him. It made me briefly appreciate the achievement of my perceived mediocrity.

Reluctant to invest in costly publicity, Robert came up with interviews on a local TV channel and the Public Broadcasting radio station, but the houses stayed dismally small. He even took me to his synagogue to schmooze the congregation there.

I had never been to Temple before, and this being a liberal synagogue, the atmosphere was friendly and relaxed. The cantor was a large attractive woman in her thirties with a thrilling singing voice and a very theatrical presence. She had seen my show and, between her 'numbers', identified me to the worshippers, telling them they should on no account miss *Shylock,* now playing at a theatre near, or at least not too far, from them, with seats available at all prices. (This unabashed mixing of the sacred and the secular is one of the things that most endears me to Jews.) The highlight of the service was the testimony of a small group of middle-aged and elderly men and women, some of them Holocaust survivors, who spoke about returning to Judaism after decades of neglecting their heritage and their faith. Their stories were so poignant, and sometimes so shocking, that for the first time I really understood how the racial and the religious could become almost indivisible, how history and faith could be inextricably connected.

*

The play limped on through an inappropriately bright and sunny April. Apart from the stage manager, who always left immediately after the show, my only companion at the theatre was a dapper ex-navy man, now retired, who acted as front-of-house manager. Declan and I didn't have much in common, excepting the tiny audiences we both had to put up with, but we would go to a bar after the show and he would talk ceaselessly about cars or baseball or nautical manoeuvres. But finally it wasn't boredom that put an end to our post-show imbibing.

'Hey, just for a change, I'll take you to the Noraid pub tomorrow. It'll be a good night because there's a fine band on before the whip-round'. He winked.

I wonder if what happened in New York a year and a half later has shaken Declan from his assumption that Irish terrorism is different from the real thing. That 'the boys' who blew up bits of London and lots of Belfast over the decades were really heroic Rob Roys, and that I would be comfortable in a pub where the whip-round, with a wink, went to finance more carnage in the place where I lived.

Americans talk about 9/11 as the end of their innocence. It was not innocence. It was that quality which resolutely distinguishes them from Europeans: naivety.

I wasn't sad when the last day of the run arrived. We had scheduled two shows in a last-ditch attempt to snare the stragglers. Between performances I was leaving the dressing room to reset my props when Declan came up the stairs.

'There's a guy here says he knows you from England.' Behind him was a slim, boyish figure, smiling broadly.

'What the f . . . ?' I remembered just in time that my visitor didn't swear.

'I'm on holiday in San Fran. Rog told me your play was on somewhere in town so I tracked you down. I thought the taxi would never find it!'

It was rather surreal to be talking to Cliff Richard, backstage in the back of beyond. Last time I had seen him, he was playing to five thousand ecstatic people at the Albert Hall. His personal manager, Rog Bruce, and I had worked in the West End years before and then lost touch. When I got recast in *The Archers* as Sean he had phoned me to say he was working for Cliff, who was a huge Ambridge fan and why didn't we all meet up for dinner.

'Will I be able to get into your show tonight?' Cliff asked.

I told him that wouldn't be a problem. He led the standing ovation at the end of the performance and the other couple of dozen brave souls joined him. Robert, my seriously out-of-pocket producer, came backstage afterwards with some friends who had constituted half the audience. Not expecting to see Cliff Richard in their midst, nobody had recognised him.

'This is . . . Cliff Richard,' I said, anticipating the gasps and that dilation of the pupils that celebrity engenders in most Americans. Everybody smiled, but nobody clutched their breast.

'Hi Clift! Are you a Brit too?' Robert was as open and friendly as he is to all strangers.

'Strictly speaking, *Sir* Cliff!' I was aghast to hear myself say. Robert loves a title.

'Hi, SIR Clift!' everybody chorused.

None of them had any idea who Cliff Richard was. He came back to Robert's house for the last-night party and was made as welcome as any friend of mine would have been. We shared a taxi downtown in the early hours, he returning to the Hyatt and I to my last night in my doss house, and I thought maybe I should apologise for my hosts' ignorance.

'Why do you think I come here on holiday?' Cliff said. 'Unless I bump into another tourist, nobody here knows who I am. It's great. The problem is that here I don't get to listen to *The Archers*. Tell me . . . has Ruth had the operation yet?'

But I was as out of touch with the programme as he. It was six months since I had recorded an episode, and I'd completely lost track of the storylines. I was about to catch up. My plane back from the States got in very early on a Sunday morning, and I was back home in plenty of time to hear the omnibus edition over an English breakfast.

Yes, Ruth had had the operation. Yes, the Grundys were surviving their latest setback. Yes, Jill was still being a saint in the kitchen. But hang on, what was Hayley saying?

'It's true then? Sean and Peter are selling up The Cat and Fiddle and moving to the West Country to open up a

B&B. We'll miss them. Shame we can't make them change their minds.'

Well, it would have been nice to be asked. The next morning, with perfect timing, there was a letter from *The Archers'* editor:

> Dear Gareth,
> This is just a note to thank you very much for your work as Sean, this time, in *The Archers.*
> We have taken the decision to write the character out because your successful touring schedule with *Shylock* (many congratulations on that, by the way) was making it impossible to progress the character in any meaningful way. In the end, we have to make room to bring on characters that we can cast on a more regular basis.
> Thank you anyway and good luck with your travels.
> Best wishes . . .

Fair enough. It was a very civil sacking, and I'm sure my long absences did contribute to Sean's dignified exit. But the character had never really caught on, either with the audience or, in all honesty, with me. In the writers' determination not to make the gay landlord a stereotype, or to give the latent homophobes of Ambridge and the wider world any real ammunition, Sean was a bit of a cipher. Vocally, I had limited myself by giving Sean an improbably deep South Welsh voice. It wasn't a vocal register very conducive to fun and, with the anodyne lines provided by the scripts, I came over as a boring boyo. In spite of my farewell episode, which culminated in a big party for me and my still tongue-tied partner Peter at The Cat and Fiddle, nobody really missed Sean.

The end of my miniscule claim to media celebrity was no great loss either. The only personal appearance I had made in my Ambridge guise had been to open a charity event in an East End gay pub where the landlord and his boyfriend were almost certainly the only people at the function who ever listened to the programme. The rest looked on in tipsy bemusement as I cracked witty in-jokes about the eccentric folk of Borsetshire. They didn't walk out, though, which may have had less to do with their forbearance than the fact that there was a male stripper on straight after me.

*

My touring schedule for *Shylock* (many congratulations on that, by the way) was promising to keep me busy for at least the next twelve months. I played a short season in London at the Hampstead Theatre and the following week, gave one-off performances in Brussels and Bangkok. In August, back in Edinburgh, playing a larger venue, there was a chance to capitalise on the previous year's success, and I donned my director's hat at the same time to launch a show called *Sherlock Holmes – The Last Act*.

It's an intriguing play by a Holmes aficionado, David Stuart Davies. In an adaptation of *The Hound of the Baskervilles* he had seen my friend Roger Llewellyn give a remarkable performance and offered to write him a solo piece. Since Sherlock Holmes without Doctor Watson is a bit like Laurel without Hardy, Roger was understandably sceptical. But by setting the action on the day of Watson's funeral, the play ingeniously gives Holmes the opportunity to return to 221B Baker Street and reminisce about his faithful friend and their exploits together. And, vulnerable in grief as he is, we get a rare glimpse of the man behind the thinking machine.

Throughout our rehearsals, I was always aware of how much I owed to Frank Barrie and what fun it was to pass on some of that experience, not to mention a few of those tricks. The play and Roger got the tremendous accolades they deserved and he looks set fair to tour the play for as long as he chooses.

When not performing himself, Roger still sometimes travels with me as my minder, often operating the lights and sound by himself, which he chooses to do manually, without the computer memory that regular technicians favour. For him, it's less like being a stage manager and more like being a conductor, responding instinctively to the pace and progress of the performance; and he is a true maestro.

Both of us are aware of how lucky we are to have found, in middle-age, roles that seem tailor-made, and from which we can make a living. Roger has a dignity, a certain reserve, almost a rectitude onstage which made him a memorable Brutus in *Julius Caesar* and makes him perfect casting for Sherlock Holmes. He is tall, with an aquiline nose, a commanding voice and razor-sharp diction.

Unlike Conan Doyle, who gave us a perfect physical description of his hero, Shakespeare, who gives nothing away, allows for a very broad spectrum of physical characteristics to fit his anti-hero. Certainly, I have the appearance of a very plausible Semite but it is much more that Shylock plays to my strengths and weaknesses as an actor. My emotional range can encompass anger, bitterness, rage, but also dignity, humour and pathos. I am as at home with verse as with prose, and have ample physical and vocal energy. What I wouldn't claim to be onstage is sexy. That 'sexiness' is an indefinable quality which cannot be acquired with any amount of effort or training. You've got it, or you haven't. The most unlikely people possess it in spades, and the most obvious candidates are completely devoid of it. It has nothing to do with looks, nothing to do with personal magnetism offstage, but somehow it speaks immediately to both sexes regardless of orientation.

If you're playing Romeo, it's half the battle. Shylock, I would venture, can get away without it.

PART THREE

Swastikas and Sadomasochism

My first professional job interview was on a bus destined for Heathrow.

The train from Hull, where I was finishing my last year at university, was over an hour late getting into London, so I arrived at the interview room, sweaty and apologetic, to find that the director had not been able to wait any longer for me and had just left for home. Home for Franz Schafranek was Vienna, and I was so desperate not to let him get away without seeing me that I pursued him to the airport-bus terminal at Victoria station.

I had accosted two or three people on the lower deck before tracking him down, and although for some reason he declined my offer to read for the part there and then, we chatted away right up until the driver started his engine. We seemed to get on really well and, with all the blazing confidence of my twenty-two years, I thought it would be only a matter of weeks before I'd be getting on another bus and riding round the Ringstrasse on my way to rehearsals at Vienna's English Speaking Theatre.

In the event, by the time I did play that theatre, the good Herr Schafranek had been long dead. His daughter Julia, who would have been a toddler when I made a prat of myself on the airport bus, invited me. She had seen *Shylock* in Edinburgh and booked me for a five-week season. Five weeks in Vienna is just about right. It's long enough to get to know the city and its glories, decide which are your favourite cafés and restaurants, and to stop feeling and behaving like a tourist. But you get to leave just

as the smugness of the place and its inhabitants are starting to sour the experience.

I opened at the end of October, a lovely time to visit
Vienna, just in time to taste the new wine and with the
weather still warm enough to go skinny-dipping in the
river. I stayed in a huge serviced apartment block about
ten minutes' walk from the theatre. Everything from the
carpets to the kitchenware was trapped in a 1950s time warp.
Retro can be camp and fun but fifties retro, especially if
you vaguely remember the dismal decade first time around,
is just drab and dispiriting. More cheerful was the positively modern seventies-style breakfast room where jolly
girls brought you wonderfully fresh coffee and boiled eggs
in quilted cosies.

It was also where you got to meet the redoubtable lady
who owned and ran the establishment. She was always
breezy and friendly in a businesslike way, her hair plaited
in tight earphones and dressed in a full skirt, white stockings and frilly blouse which I took for a sort of national
costume. It was all very 'von Trapp' and, given that she was
well into her seventies, alarming and disarming in equal
measure.

Her husband was even older and sightings of him were
rarer. But every time I did spot him, I fear I might have been
guilty of staring. Another English actor, who had worked
at the theatre before me, claimed to know a little of his
history. He had been, I was told, the chief vet at the famous
Spanish Riding Academy in Vienna. It was one of the few
tourist sights in the city that I never got to see, I suppose
because horses drilled into walking sideways to Strauss has
limited appeal for me. But Adolf Hitler had been a great
fan and frequent visitor, and looking at mine host, it
seemed more than likely that he would have been in charge
of the horse pills around the same time that Austria was

annexed so effortlessly by the Nazis. I'd love to have known if they met and what they talked about.

Austrian elections were held during my stay in Vienna and one in four voters chose the neo-Nazi party of Joerg Haider. The people I was working with at the theatre were distressed and despondent at the outcome, but there was no denying that parts of the country were exulting at the revival of the far right. Because of agreements with the Allies at the end of World War Two, Austria wasn't occupied by troops in the way that Germany was. Without such a constant reminder of their crimes and their defeat, there does not seem to have been the same self-examination and remorse about the past.

Vienna, of course, still revels in one part of its history, the rule of the Emperor Franz Josef and his wife Sisi. They are celebrated everywhere from portraits in cafés to kitsch mementos in the souvenir shops. It's more comfortable to represent the era when Vienna was capital of the old Austro-Hungarian Empire and predominant in music and the arts, than the more shameful recent past.

Before the annexation in 1938, the Anschluss, the Jewish population of Vienna was at a peak of one hundred and eighty-five thousand. Seven years later, only about eight hundred Jews remained: those who had managed to stay hidden until the end of the war. Of the forty-two synagogues which were functioning before the war, only one escaped unravaged, because the building looked residential and went unnoticed by the Nazis. From being major contributors to the cultural and scientific life of the city and the Austro-Hungarian Empire, Jews were reduced to the status of pariahs, forced to scrub the streets, denied all civil liberties, expelled from most professions and forced to wear the Jew Badge. Of the sixty-five thousand deported to concentration camps only two thousand survived.

But before I learnt all these gruesome facts from my visits to the hugely impressive Jewish Museum and the Simon Wiesenthal Documentation Centre, I had the comparatively minor trauma of opening my play. It was still warm enough on the first night to have a champagne reception in the garden of the British Embassy residence, which, like most things in Vienna, had an old-fashioned formality. But among the other, rather sober guests, I was introduced to a very glamorous Austrian ex-film actress of a certain age. She was the sort who used to crop up in the Hammer Horror films in a low-cut dress and big hair as one of Dracula's early victims. You remembered her because she was the only one in the film to have anything approaching what you imagined to be a real Transylvanian accent. She'd spent time in Hollywood and was witty and gossipy, especially about some of the other people at the party. She was very complimentary too about the show.

'But I'm so glad you didn't go on and on about the Holocaust, my darling . . . We're really fed up to the back teeth with that by now.' Minutes later, I found myself chatting to a much older lady, who turned out to be a survivor of the Holocaust they were all allegedly so fed up with.

'You got one thing very wrong, you know,' she said, in excellent English. 'When you mentioned the yellow star of David, you placed your hand on your upper arm. Quite wrong. That's where the Nazis wore their swastikas. We always wore the star over our hearts . . . ' – she took the champagne glass from me and placed my right hand across my chest – ' . . . so.'

I made sure at the next and every subsequent performance to rectify the error.

On my first night off, I got the chance to go and see someone else perform onstage. Gregory Peck. He was the guest star of an extravaganza billed as *Vienna Salutes*

America in the glorious Musikverein concert hall. The orchestra and soloists gave us lots of Gershwin and Strauss, and there were jolly songs and love duets from musicals and operettas. Mr Peck entered. The blue-blackness of his hair and beard only slightly diminished the impact of his venerable presence. Abandoning his walking stick as he approached the podium, he delivered Lincoln's Gettysburg address to a totally captivated audience. He pitched it perfectly, his timing immaculate and his phrasing faultless. I think it must have been one of his last engagements.

Almost as memorable were the other stars of the show, onstage together for the first time ever: the Vienna Boys' Choir and the Boys' Choir of Harlem, New York. The all-black American lads stood ramrod straight, and when not singing, smiled fixedly at their public. Their Viennese counterparts had a more relaxed, professional attitude, but when they sang together, it was the sweetest sound. I couldn't help wondering what some of the grandfathers of those Austrian choristers might have thought about such a harmonious partnership.

*

'I am Xaviera. You will perform your play in Amsterdam.'

Not sure if it was a question or a statement, I put the tone down to her being Dutch, but I should have been warned. Xaviera Hollander wrote a book in the early seventies called *The Happy Hooker*, about her career as a brothel-keeper in New York. It was made into a film starring Lynn Redgrave: 'About as sexy as a kipper, dahling' was Xaviera's verdict. Whatever other careers she had embraced since then, she was now being an impresario.

We met at the Edinburgh Festival. She was big, blonde and bossy, and at the time I thought rather intriguing.

Months later, she got in touch to offer dates, and a ludicrously low fee. There were effusive e-mail messages about how the paucity of the remuneration would be more than compensated for by the richness of my entertainment. I was to stay in her luxurious home in the centre of Amsterdam, 'feeding off the finest foods and drinking of the best wines'. The alternative to a week of the high life in Amsterdam in mid-November was the customary low life of Shepherd's Bush. So I went.

At Schiphol airport, a curious pair of young women had waited patiently while the customs official searched my wretched trunk again. One was chubby, bespectacled and very chatty and the other frizzy-haired, lanky and rather scared-looking, as if someone had just struck her. In the whole week I spent in Holland, I never heard her speak. Xaviera had sent two of her 'X Team' to collect me, along with one of her two butlers, who also drove, cooked, chain-smoked and, by the look of his shaking hands, drank a lot.

I felt a pang of disappointment when the house turned out to be a solid suburban-looking villa and not the high-gabled canal-side residence of my imagination. Xaviera, caftan-clad, greeted me, rather imperiously I thought, and ordered her second butler, a pretty Filipino boy, to take me to my room. At the threshold, he took a tissue from his pocket and dextrously and without comment removed a small dog turd from the carpet. Downstairs, the chauffeur-butler-lush served the first of several meals that would strain anyone's perception of what constitutes the finest foods and the best wines whilst Xaviera presided over the table like a duchess, or maybe like a brothel-keeper, barking her

orders and talking endlessly about herself and the noto-
riety she assumed she still enjoyed.

The venue for my performances was a tiny room at the
back of an antique shop which was transformed into a
sort of supper club in the evenings. My shows began after
the wining and dining at about 10.30, by which time the
audience could be forgiven for being a bit weary or a little
drunk or both. This wouldn't matter if my show had been
a cabaret turn, but although I'm delighted that *Shylock*
does usually get a good few laughs, I would never claim it
was ideal after-dinner entertainment.

There was a speech from Xaviera before the show,
another brief one at the interval and, as I took my calls,
she disappeared momentarily and came back with a
bunch of chrysanthemums which she thrust at me and
then made another speech. I stood behind her feeling like
a schoolboy at the annual speech day, being praised by the
headmistress. The show had gone well, but there was a
definite feeling that it was Xaviera's evening.

After changing, I came out to meet her guests. 'This is
Otto, one of my best lovers,' she said, summoning me over
to meet a distinguished elderly gentleman who wasn't re-
motely fazed by the introduction. She made 'one of my
best lovers' sound as sexy as one of her best clogs, and I
wondered whether, for all the frankness and explicit talk,
sex to Xaviera wasn't still a business. But most of the
Dutch people I met gave off the same aura of earnest
detachment. It wasn't only sex either: most subjects got a
similarly lacklustre response. Maybe it's that Netherlanders
don't need to invoke passion because it's an inappropriate
reaction when you are always right about everything.

'Where are the flowers?' Xaviera asked at the end of the
evening. I had left them backstage to brighten up what

passed for a dressing room. 'Fetch them. They must go back in the vase.'

My first-night bouquet had been filched from one of the dining tables, and it appeared nightly thereafter before the curtain speech. When we got back to the house, Xaviera got some guilders from a strongbox and put them in my hand.

'For tonight,' she said. 'Well done. The same for each performance.' I know acting is the second oldest profession but I have never felt quite so much like a tart.

To cheer myself up, the next day I went to the Anne Frank Museum. In the cold autumn drizzle, I joined the long line of tourists that snaked around the canal-side building. With about half-a-million visitors a year, the queue is a permanent feature, but it was a chatty, good-humoured wait. Inside, the chatting stopped. The house where Anne Frank hid from the Nazis with her family and four other Jews for two years before her capture and death in a concentration camp is a very sobering place. The rooms are emptied of furniture. Documents, photographs and a few significant objects are displayed along with quotes from Anne's famous diary. Video screens put the whole story in a historical perspective, and as you leave there is a café, bookstore and souvenir shop. It is beautifully presented, and one is constantly aware of the skill in its execution. But I was strangely unaffected by the experience, as if the very professionalism of the exhibit somehow divested it of the power to move.

The Hollandse Schouwburg or Dutch Theatre was for me a much more potent monument. From being one of the most important theatres in Amsterdam before the war, it was renamed the Jewish Theatre under German occupation and only Jewish performers were allowed to entertain their exclusively Jewish audience. In 1942, it became an assembly point for Jews who were to be deported. In the years that followed, the theatre saw between sixty and eighty thousand men, women and children sent to the death camps. Across the road from the theatre is a school building. Here the citizens of Amsterdam risked their lives by smuggling Jewish children to safety.

The Dutch, I discovered, had been ambivalent towards the Jews in their midst, and there were certainly collaborators as well as heroes. But even those not disposed to like them were outraged by the Nazis' brutality. One old lady in my audience told me wryly of graffiti she had seen as a child during the war. Translated, it read: 'Get your dirty hands off OUR dirty Jews!'

I never confronted Xaviera about her attitude to me as a person or as a performer, although I was offended by both. I told myself it was politeness that held me back, but I suspected it was cowardice. It worried me that I had been so passive when I could so easily have told her what I thought and thereby resolved the rather frosty relationship that had prevailed throughout my stay.

Soon after I got back to London I bumped into Kerry Shale, a hugely experienced and talented solo performer, who I knew had also done the Happy Hooker's gig. I told him about my experience and how it had left me feeling. He just laughed.

'Did you ever get to see her bedroom?' he asked. I hadn't. 'There's this huge photo over the bed of a young man with his mouth wide open. He's drinking a stream of piss from a woman squatting above him. That's Xaviera!'

He had cottoned on early to the fact that she was, maybe because of her early career choice, a dominatrix who surrounded herself with willing slaves: the 'X Team', the butlers, the boyfriends. No one would call me naive about sex but I had honestly never understood that Xaviera was role-playing her sadism as professionally and as sincerely as I hoped I was performing in *Shylock*. Unfortunately, I had failed to realise either that we were in a play together, or what my part in it was. From the moment I arrived, I had been horribly miscast.

The Case for Shylock

In any live show you gauge the success or failure of your performance by the audience's reaction. Laughter and applause are the most obvious rewards, but for the parts of a script where neither is appropriate there is another even more gratifying reaction: silence. And the sounds of silence can be quite different. A totally Gentile audience often comes to my play even less prepared than I had been before starting my researches. Their silence is often of shock or disbelief. An exclusively Jewish audience is more challenging. Not only are they with you all the way, they are frequently several steps ahead. Their silence is of remembrance and recognition.

For my first totally Jewish audience I went to the right place, Israel, as a participant in the annual Habima Theatre Festival in December 2000. It was not the best of times when Roger Llewellyn, the maestro, and I arrived. But neither was it the worst. The performances in Haifa and Tel Aviv went ahead as scheduled, but the shows in Jerusalem were cancelled for security reasons, and we were advised not even to visit the city. This was a major disappointment as Jerusalem had featured so significantly in my Christian childhood and, of course, in the history of Shylock's people.

From the Holy Places to the Wailing Wall, I had some notion of what I had missed in Jerusalem. Tel Aviv, on the other hand, came as a complete surprise, not least because there is barely a building evident in the city more than fifty years old. Also I was expecting to be surrounded by the pale and prayer-curled Hassidim, their wives in pull-on wigs, that I had seen pouring off the El Al flights at Heathrow, or populating certain areas of north London. I was quite unprepared for the very secular, vibrant, sometimes aggressive populace.

Israelis, in their own capital city, are amongst the least civil people I have ever met. A smile to a stranger is rarely returned, and if you are lucky enough to get a prompt answer to a question, it will most likely be a blunt monosyllable. And yet, when you get introduced to some locals, even on the most casual basis, they are nearly always demonstrative and often tactile. Social intercourse with a total stranger on the street, or in shops or hotel foyers is evidently thought of as a waste of hospitable energy. After a day or two, you find yourself not minding, and by the end of a week, you are almost competing over the level of indifference you can display. But the energy and dynamism are infectious too. People everywhere seem to be working and playing at speed, charging around in pursuit of some unspecified deadline, fuelled by the certitude that nothing lasts for ever.

The afterlife, it had to be explained to me, means something very different to Jews than the concept of a Christian heaven where rewards await those who have lived virtuous lives. To Jews, what matters is what you do and how you do it on earth. That put much of the Jewish experience as I witnessed it into a clearer perspective and certainly helped me to understand their homeland.

This tiny manufactured state is so crammed with diversity that every opinion formed is almost immediately confounded. In Israel, I heard kids making bad-taste, but very funny jokes about the Holocaust survivors they met in supermarkets, and I struck up a conversation with a man on the beach in front of our hotel who said he looked

forward to an imminent Armageddon with his Arab neighbours as an appropriate end to history.

There were people who saw the political aspects of my
show as a righteous indictment of the hatred and persecution that has dogged the Jew through the millennia. There
were others who saw that the marginalisation and repression of any minority is likely to have ugly consequences,
and that their own country was now engaged in just such
repression. Even among my all Jewish audiences, I discerned
the different sounds of silence.

My biggest fear was how they would react to a non-Jew
tackling issues so particular to themselves. At a party, a
woman did ask me whether or not I thought it was 'pre-
sumptuous' to assume a Jewish identity, as I do in the narrative parts of my play. A bit taken aback by the way she had
phrased the question, I waffled something about an actor
having to identify totally with the characters he is playing.
It turned out she was not being confrontational but had
recently converted to Judaism before her marriage to an
Israeli diplomat and had some insecurities of her own.

Obviously her conversion had been voluntary but it
made me think again about the trial scene in *The Merchant*
and the sequence leading up to Shylock's enforced conversion to Christianity. After Portia has cheated Shylock of
his pound of flesh by pointing out that the bond between
him and Antonio does not include 'one drop of Christian
blood', the court exults in her brilliant victory. Shylock,
wisely knowing when it's time to quit, makes to leave the
courtroom. He says:

> Why, then the devil give him good of it!
> I'll stay no longer question.

But Portia stops him:

> Tarry, Jew.
> The law hath yet another hold on you.
> It is enacted in the laws of Venice,
> If it be proved against an alien
> That by direct or indirect attempts
> He seek the life of any citizen,
> The party 'gainst the which he doth contrive
> Shall seize one half his goods; the other half
> Comes to the privy coffer of the state;
> And the offender's life lies in the mercy
> Of the Duke only, 'gainst all other voice.
> In which predicament, I say, thou stand'st: . . .
> Down, therefore, and beg mercy of the Duke.

Everyone has to be relieved that Shylock's grotesque vengeance has been thwarted, but by forcing him to kneel and beg for the Duke's clemency, Portia is hardly true to her most famous injunction:

> The quality of mercy is not strained;
> It droppeth as the gentle rain from heaven
> Upon the place beneath . . .

She has also made plain that it is Shylock's status as 'an alien' in the Venetian State that makes him uniquely vulnerable to its separatist laws. Moments later, when Antonio is called upon by the Duke to be the final arbiter of Shylock's fate, he forgives him the financial penalties due to himself but insists that half of Shylock's wealth be given to Lorenzo, 'the gentleman that lately stole his daughter.' That is galling enough, but there is worse to come. This deal is only on condition that Shylock converts to Christianity.

Commentaries on the play point out that, in his own terms, Antonio is being munificent in offering Shylock the chance of salvation through Jesus Christ. But it doesn't play that way in the theatre. It comes across as the final humiliation, the last proof, if it were needed, of the Christian characters' contempt and disrespect for Shylock and his people. Whatever an audience may think of Shylock up to that point, it is almost impossible to withhold some sympathy from him then.

A forced conversion reminded me of the aversion therapy treatment that was offered to gay men in the twentieth century as an alternative to prosecution for their deviant lifestyle. Underlying the professed and inappropriate compassion was the same ignorance and intolerance of difference that manifests itself in religious prejudice. I may not know what it is to be a Jew or to experience anti-Semitism, but at the time that my sexuality was becoming evident to me, it was still illegal to give it expression. Surrounded by the disapproval and the pressures of society and one's peers to conform, it is easy to understand the attraction of a cure, an escape route. A suppression of natural instincts, a profession of change, the living of a lie can all seem preferable options to the hostility of the rest of the world.

'Art thou contented, Jew? What dost thou say?' asks Portia after Antonio makes his offer. Shylock answers: 'I am content'. Seconds later, he leaves the courtroom and the play forever. Those three words encapsulate for me the enigma of Shylock. Will he leave the court, go straight to confirmation class and begin his rehabilitation? Or has he learnt from the lessons of history that survival for him and his race demands a degree of pragmatism? Three simple words; but how they are spoken and whether they are meant to be taken at face value is the key to the destiny of that troubled and troublesome man.

*

The theatre scene in Israel, largely indebted to its early Russian influence, is eclectic, dynamic and popular. As part of an international festival of one-person shows, we had the advantage of a beautifully equipped and intimate theatre as well as the services of a skilled and helpful technical team. One of them, a young man called Jacob, who had just finished his compulsory stint in the Israeli army, took Roger and me backstage to look for the few pieces of furniture I use in the show. We soon found what we needed amidst the vast clutter of chairs and tables that could have furnished any drama from ancient Babylon to 1950s Brooklyn and beyond. Picking our way back through the labyrinthine store rooms, we passed by the smaller properties: table lamps, vases, samovars, birdcages and the like. In one corner was a collection of hatboxes, handbags and suitcases of various sizes.

In *Shylock*, my final exit is a slow walk offstage along a narrow corridor of light towards a blazing spotlight in the wings. I carry a small attaché case. The image is of a disillusioned and disenfranchised Shylock walking doggedly towards his future. It is a deliberately ambiguous image; the audience must make up its own mind as to whether he has a future, or what that future might be.

I paused at the pile of luggage and breathed in that intriguing smell of old and well-travelled leather. My eye had caught a battered, little black case with reinforced corners. Picking it up, it seemed almost weightless. It was not made of leather at all but some shiny compressed material, and I could just make out written below the metal handle: 'Garantiert echt Amerikanische Vulcan-Fibre.' I found myself asking Jacob if I could use it in the play. He seemed dubious. There was a little yellow sticker taped on the front with a four digit number on it.

'I think it's used in one of the shows we keep in repertoire,' he said. 'But I'll ask.'

In the dressing room on my first night in Tel Aviv, along
with an exotic bouquet and a glossy book in Hebrew
about the history of the National Theatre which, of course,
I had to pretend to read backwards, was the scruffy little
case. I took it onstage with me. When the performances
were over, I managed to persuade Jacob's boss to swap the
'Vulcan Fibre' case for my much more serviceable leather
one, and it has never missed a performance since.

I am genuinely not sentimental or superstitious about
props, but when I pick up that ancient, empty object,
probably pre-war, with its German legend under my fist,
to make Shylock's last exit from the stage, it feels suddenly
very weighty, with a secret legacy that I am fortunate
enough only to guess at.

On a practical level, of course, my lightweight memento
from Israel makes good sense at airport check-ins. Over
the years, I have jettisoned some of my heavier costumes
or swapped bulky props for lighter alternatives so that now
I tip the scales just a kilo or two above the permitted maxi-
mum. Only the most mean-minded operative will bother
to charge me excess baggage. But travelling to Romania on
Tarom, the national airline, I was asked to pay for my
paltry extra pounds. I put it down to their desperation for
foreign currency, but I was not about to surrender my
track record for zero charges. I opened the stage trunk
and, much to the fury of passengers waiting in line behind
me, started to dress up in the first things that came to hand:
a woollen waistcoat, a thick black gabardine, a battered
homburg over a skull cap, a prayer shawl over my shoulders and a huge turquoise ring on my finger. I scraped by
with a few grams to spare. At security, I emptied my

pockets of money and keys and stepped confidently through the screening arch. The alarm went off. I retreated, removed my metal-buckled belt and my chunk of costume jewellery and passed through again in silence. Only two days later, at the dress rehearsal in the Transylvanian city of Sibiu, did I realise I had left the ring behind at Heathrow. Thinking it would make little difference, I decided to mime it. But it was not the same. For the first time, I realised the importance of that bauble to my alter ego.

*

Every Shylock will find for himself the moment when the determination to be revenged on Antonio becomes truly implacable. For some performers, it is during the first aside in his opening scene:

> If I can catch him once upon the hip,
> I will feed fat the ancient grudge I bear him.

This is a perfectly justifiable reading but it gives Shylock rather a single-track journey en route to the trial scene. For other actors, it is the elopement of Jessica and the theft of his money and jewels that turn his desire for vengeance into an absolute resolve. But this is harder to signal to an audience because his first reactions to that news are reported rather than witnessed. For me, it is the wanton behaviour of his only child in Genoa, the callous surrender of his turquoise ring, which marks the point of no return. And this betrayal is revealed to him by Tubal in his only scene. Tubal has returned from Genoa with the bad news that he has not been able to trace the eloping couple, Lorenzo and Jessica, but with the good news that Antonio's business ventures have almost certainly gone bust, rendering him vulnerable to Shylock's revenge. He might have left it at that but, for whatever motive, he goes on to give Shylock more details than may be strictly necessary:

> TUBAL Your daughter spent in Genoa, as I heard, one night, fourscore ducats.
> SHYLOCK Thou stick'st a dagger in me. I shall never see my gold again. Fourscore ducats at a sitting, fourscore ducats!

That news has obviously infuriated Shylock, so Tubal goes on to sugar the pill with an assurance he knows will go down well:

> TUBAL There came divers of Antonio's creditors in my company to Venice that swear he cannot choose but break.
> SHYLOCK I am very glad of it. I'll plague him; I'll torture him. I am glad of it.

Maybe Tubal should have quit while he was ahead, but no, he puts his head back in the lion's mouth:

> TUBAL One of them showed me a ring he had of your daughter for a monkey.
> SHYLOCK Out upon her! Thou torturest me, Tubal. It was my turquoise; I had it of Leah when I was a bachelor . . .

Jessica has not only stolen the betrothal ring given to Shylock by his dead wife, but she has exchanged it for a monkey. Something so precious, given away in return for something so trivial. And to Shakespeare's audience, and to Shylock, a monkey would have had another significance; it was a symbol of sexual licence, a reminder that his virgin daughter was or soon would be making the beast with two backs with a Gentile opportunist. Shylock goes on:

> SHYLOCK ... I would not have given it for a wilderness of monkeys.

Deciding whether to play those lines as defiant or defeated, furious or tearful is one of those choices that can keep an actor awake at night. It could be the moment when the audience returns its verdict on your Shylock.

Lost in Translation

'A wilderness of monkeys' is one of the most evocative and extraordinary images in the whole of Shakespeare. It conjures up something so chaotic and yet so desolate, so teeming and yet so empty, that it defies the visual imagination. My play has been translated into Catalan, Spanish, Italian, Russian, Dutch and French but none of those languages has come up with a satisfactory equivalent of that line. The translators have used 'forest of monkeys', 'jungle of monkeys' even 'trees full of monkeys', but the resonances that the line has in English simply elude them.

Translators take a justifiable pride in their skill but sometimes they are quite hard to convince about the right choice of word. Part of their job as they see it, and part of the tradition of European writing, is to avoid the repetition of a word and demonstrate the richness of their vocabulary by finding a synonym. Once you have got them to concede that English has the largest vocabulary in the world, you have to convince them that Shakespeare uses the word 'mercy' five times in Portia's 'quality of mercy' speech, not because he cannot think of an alternative, but because the very repetition of the word is what gives it its potency.

*

In Montreal, that most welcoming and generous-spirited of bilingual cities, some performances were given with a simultaneous translation over headphones into French.

My show moves at a hell of a pace, and the actor who read the script from inside his small glass booth, would emerge looking shell-shocked and exhausted. He reckoned that for every five English words in my script, he had to squeeze in eight French. In Mexico, we used a different system for the Spanish translation: surtitles. That was never plain sailing either. There was a very highly-strung technical duo, with one operator to decide when the translated line should be projected above the stage and another who was then supposed to press the right button. Sometimes I would be in full flow, and come to a line which always gets a laugh in any country. Silence. There would be a distant Hispanic hissing in the circle, and, several seconds after I had moved on to more solemn matters, a huge guffaw. The sulking that went on from either or both of our temperamental operators over supper became known as the Mexican stand-off.

The first time another actor played *Shylock* was in Spain. But in Barcelona, Manel Barcelo chose to premiere the show in his native Catalan. Manel is, in fact, the perfect Tubal: slightly built with gradually receding hair and a face that suggests warmth, a mild bewilderment and a sly sense of humour. He is immensely quick-witted, vocally and physically mercurial and sometimes takes you by surprise with the passion of his opinions. Onstage, he is engaging in a thoroughly effortless way that makes me quite envious. I find it easier to get under the scratchy skin of Shylock than to don the gentler mantle of his best friend.

In rehearsals it became obvious that Manel viewed *Shylock* as a much more political play than I had conceived it. What I had written in response to playing a complex classical role had, in the hands of a different actor, become his interpretation of my response. Understandably, he didn't share my obsession with the nuances of Shakespeare's language, and the extracts from *The Merchant* were suddenly illustrative rather than pivotal. He knew his audience would feel the same way.

He had little English, and I no Spanish. In between us was our director, Luca Valentino. Whilst waiting for the Italian connection to get its act together in Venice, Luca had swiftly set up this production, which would go on to win Manel a clutch of awards and a thrilling tour all over South America. Luca is a multi-talented and perceptive director and also a gentle and persuasive man, both in and out of the theatre. Even in his second language, he established a fluent and profound dialogue with Manel about the play and then tried to explain it to me in his fourth language, English. Between them, they convinced me that what I had written was really too Anglo-centric and that a little rewriting would strengthen the play's arguments and give it more relevance for the Barcelona audience. In fact, the rewrites we collaborated on were an improvement in any language and are now permanent fixtures when I perform the show myself.

In production, the changes to the play are, of course, not just textual. As a director, Luca has a very different visual sense from Frank's or my own. In the Spanish version, the stage is totally empty. Manel enters with a large leather suitcase which has been ingeniously designed not only to contain all his costumes and props but also to become whatever furniture a scene might require. At one point it turns into the plush seating of a Venetian gondola, at another it becomes the repository of all Shylock's wealth.

My play is full of references to great English actors of the past who have tackled Shylock. Most of their names mean very little to non-English audiences, but the anecdotes associated with them have a universal appeal. I tell the story of Henry Irving inserting an entirely invented scene into *The Merchant of Venice* which has nothing to do with Shakespeare's text, but went a long way to gaining sympathy for Irving's interpretation. Whilst Shylock has been dining reluctantly with Antonio, Bassanio and the rest, his daughter Jessica has eloped with Lorenzo, compounding the deed by stealing her father's money and jewels. Irving interpolated a scene in dumb show when Shylock returns to his house and discovers his loss. Irving's productions were famous for their lavishness, and this new scene was no exception.

There was a long wall upstage with a canal behind it, a little ship moored and, in the distance, the beautiful outline of the Doge's Palace. Stairs from upstage centre led to a little bridge beyond which was the entrance to Shylock's house. Ellen Terry, who famously partnered Irving as a magnificent Portia, described the scene: 'The stage was empty, desolate, with no light but a pale moon, and all sounds of life at a great distance.' There is the tapping of a walking stick offstage, and the weary Jew appears at the top of the stairs, carrying a lantern. He descends, then crosses the bridge and taps with his stick on the front door of his house. There is no response. He knocks again. Still, no answer. He raises his lantern to his darkened upper windows and, as the realisation dawns, his features register a look of dumb and complete despair. Curtain.

A scene without language that would speak volumes in any language. But it was not a convention unique to Irving. Luca's production drew on a European tradition of playing that scene which has a daring that even the great Irving might have envied. To the strains of an old recording of *Rigoletto*, Manel enters slightly tipsily, struggles to find his keys, abandons the attempt and knocks on his front door. No answer. So he calls out:

'Jessica!'

He calls out 'Jessica' not once, but fifty times. Each call different: affectionate, impatient, angry, cajoling, worried, desperate, lonely, terrified and so on and on. Fifty different emotions, each one distinct, each one resonant, each one chilling and pitiful.

The first time I saw it in rehearsal, I was quite speechless. It is a technical feat that put me in awe, and one that I have never dared to try and copy. Yet.

Bloodsuckers

They wanted us to know that they had searched our luggage. The hotel bedroom door we had so carefully locked was left unlocked and our suitcases, though still closed, had obviously had their contents moved. People were very nervous about talking to us, or at least of being seen talking to us. There was one lad though, who was very chatty, and offered to walk me and Fanny back to the hotel after our performance at his university. En route, he never stopped asking questions about British weather, food, transport systems, gross national product and the Royal Family. He didn't seem all that interested in the answers (although he was missing a golden opportunity, as Fanny is a world expert on the House of Windsor). When we reached the reception desk, he stopped in mid-sentence, thanked us for the pleasure of our company and disappeared.

Staff at the British Embassy told us later that the youth would have been assigned to us that day and instructed to make sure we returned straight from work to the hotel, talking to no one but himself.

In the early 1980s, cultural relations between Romania and the UK, though not easy, were still possible. The programmes of Dylan Thomas and Shakespeare that Fanny and I were offering were sufficiently safe fare for us to have been invited on a short Eastern European tour. We had been rather spoilt by Hungary, which seemed to bear its communist yoke with at least a veneer of ironic humour, and we thought Poland had been a bit grim by comparison. Nothing however could have prepared us for Ceausescu's fiefdom.

As well as Bucharest, we went west to perform in the universities of Timisoara, Cluj, and Iasi in the north-east. Transport was in ancient and lethal-looking Russian aeroplanes, or trains designed for terminal discomfort. Impressions were not improved by our travelling companion, the cultural attachée from the British Embassy. A plump redhead in her late twenties, she had spent two years in Romania and had evidently hated every minute of it. Every time we spotted what seemed like a redeeming feature, she just snorted her derision and marched on. Most striking was the fact that no Romanian would catch our eye or, if they did, they looked away again immediately. Officials, academics, theatre workers, hotel staff all appeared to be in mortal fear of something.

Ten years later, the object of that fear stood on a balcony with his monstrous wife and heard the crowd starting, at last, to vent their fury on him. The expression of disbelief and then the dawning realisation on his face that his game was up is, for me, the most dramatic and memorable moment from that astonishing period of history. I have never wanted to see the film of the execution of Nicolae and Elena Ceausescu, but I have since met Romanians for whom it is favourite viewing.

Strictly speaking, by the way, that should be Sir Nicolae and Lady Elena. When it was thought politically advantageous to keep the tyrant happy, the Queen was advised to confer an honorary knighthood on Ceausescu and to agree to his request to stay overnight at Buckingham Palace during his state visit. I am a half-hearted republican, but even a volunteer tumbrel driver would find some sympathy for the poor woman for having to put up with that. It would be like lending your toothbrush to Dracula.

Transylvanians, I was told during my first visit there, were scornful of the association with that fictional

Western icon. The true Dracula, Vlad the Impaler, was a very different creature from Bram Stoker's creation or later movie manifestations. On my second visit, this time with *Shylock*, I was shown the sight where a vast theme park dedicated to the famous vampire was to be constructed, at enormous cost, to attract much-needed tourism. Free market capitalism had overcome the Transylvanians' cultural sensibilities.

A friend had spent a year in Bucharest during the 1960s, researching his PhD. I asked him how he had survived in such a repressive atmosphere for so long without going mad. He hadn't. In his desperation to get out, he had started shouting at people in the street until the authorities took him in and eventually arranged his repatriation. To call Stephen Davies a polymath is a bit like describing Leonardo as a good all-rounder. His double first at Oxford, his doctorate, his jobs as literary agent, editor, TV producer, scriptwriter and numberless excursions into academe, as well as the arts and the media have given him a CV that would make Jeffrey Archer blush. His interests are as limitless as his curiosity. He has learnt more about more things than anyone I know. And he remembers all of it.

This should make him insufferable, but he is the easiest and most delightful company imaginable. He is happy to share his erudition with you but never uses it as a weapon to reinforce his intellectual superiority. As much as architecture, obscure operas and computer gizmos, he loves a good gossip. Not surprisingly, when he was about to graduate from Oxford, the Secret Service were anxious to talk to him. He might have turned out to be a notable spy, but when he volunteered to his recruiter that he was the university's most incorrigible gossip, MI5 suddenly lost interest.

As a tour manager, Stephen is not obvious casting; he is as likely as I am to have forgotten where the airline tickets are, or to have left the prompt script behind on the kitchen table. He wouldn't lay claim to the unflappability which is usually associated with stage management, but nobody could fault him either for his willingness to learn new skills or the rapport he achieves with theatre technicians all over the world. We have toured together to Belgium, Ukraine, India, Greece, Portugal, the States and dozens of dates in England, but it was in Romania where Stephen really came into his own; the British Council can't have sent many tours out there where half the company spoke Romanian.

The first theatres we played at Piatra Neamt and Sibiu were well-established venues, regularly hosting international festivals, but it was the chasm between our expectations and the reality of their ancient technical equipment that took us by surprise. Not to mention some of their working methods, which would send a British health-and-safety inspector into orbit. The Soviet-era time warp was reinforced by the presence backstage of three personal dressers for me. Even one dresser is *de trop* as my costumes are necessarily simple and few, but we all somehow managed to look busy in the run-up to the show, finding loose buttons and re-ironing creaseless shirts. Not even lousy wages, lethal working conditions, and poor job security seem able to diminish Romanian theatre workers' good humour and pride in what they do.

In the West, our images of Romania are overwhelmingly of orphans, child AIDS victims, or the mentally-ill, hidden away for decades in appalling conditions. These are the legacy of their hideous past, when there was little reason for hope and every reason for secrecy. But there is another reality: that of a country at last getting to like itself again. Particularly amongst the young, there is now a self-assurance, not to be confused with arrogance, that is very impressive. It manifests itself in the pride they take in their own culture, which they don't seem over-eager to swap for a Big Mac and a pair of designer trainers, and even in their body language. Romanian youth stands up straight, and looks you in the eye.

In Iasi, a major city in the north-east, close to the Moldovan border, I went back to the English Department at the university to give a talk to the students. Superficial changes since the 1980s, like the kindergarten turquoise and lilac paint which had replaced the regulation dark brown and cream on the corridor walls, were only the beginning. I remembered vividly those stilted encounters with the nervous students, exchanging only the most unambiguous pleasantries with the faculty, and the relief when the sessions were finally over. This time, the talk and the challenging question-and-answer session were over all too soon. In the staff room afterwards, over coffee and pastries, the Head of Department lamented that classes were finishing early that day because the students were coming out on strike to protest about their allowances. Try as he might, he couldn't keep the note of pride out of his voice.

If the young are distancing themselves from the horrors of the past, other sections of society seem quite prepared to confront them. Iasi has a grim reputation as the place where Adolf Eichmann had notable success with his policy of Jewish extermination in the Second World War. In spite, or maybe because of that, it is also the city which hosts an annual Yiddish Theatre Festival.

The Festival honours Avram Goldfaden, a prolific playwright and director who founded the first Jewish theatre in Iasi in 1876. There were plays, concerts, musicals, workshops, seminars and several rather dispiritingly termed monodramas. It is a very popular and competitive genre

in Eastern Europe and I was quite relieved that my mono-
drama was to be the final show of the Festival. More or less
free for six days, Stephen and I had the chance to see lots
of other people's work, and even play truant for forty-
eight hours to go sightseeing. Not surprisingly, Stephen's
appetite for sights and wonders is insatiable. (I, on the
other hand, think you can have too much of a good thing.)
We could not be in northern Romania, he insisted, and
not see the painted monasteries of Bucovina.

'How many of them are there?' I asked, guardedly.

'I'm afraid we'll only have time for five or six,' Stephen
said.

It was towards the end of October, but in Bucovina the
first, early snows of winter had just fallen. The conifers
hung onto their fresh covering, but the deciduous trees
would yield theirs to the slightest gust of wind, revealing
glorious patchworks of ochre and red on the white of the
hillsides. The tourist season was over, and we found ourselves wandering around the monasteries, virtually alone.
I have seen my fair share of frescoes painted on church
walls, but always on the inside. In Bucovina, it is the ex-
terior walls that are covered in the most vivid and graphic
Christian imagery. There is a lot of violent and bloodthirsty storytelling that put me in mind of that painted
screen in Loddon Church, depicting the alleged murder of
little William of Norwich, but many of the faces are
memorable for their gentleness and serenity.

It was a Sunday, so we were able to overhear some of the
Orthodox services. Most of the monasteries we visited are
inhabited by nuns, and they manage to defy their forbidding and all-embracing black habits with ruddy, smiling
faces, sparkling eyes and an aura that could almost make
you believe they were onto something. Where we found

monks, they were much more austere and their singing, though impressive, seemed to lack the joy that the women brought to their harmonies.

We stayed overnight in a splendidly eccentric bed-and-breakfast establishment called 'Lulu's'. The name suggests somewhere rather louche, but Lulu's had rock-hard beds, alarming wiring and a jolly proprietress (Lulu?) who announced that she was just off to an all-night wedding party, and left us to our own devices, well supplied with roast pork, Romanian polenta and smoky red wine.

Bucovina was unmissable. Back at the Festival, I'm not sure whether we had been missed or not. In the manner of Eastern European theatre festivals, all participants were billeted in a standard-class hotel just a few minutes' walk from the theatre. Set meals were served, strictly in exchange for tokens distributed by the organisers and, whilst most mealtime conversations were conducted in Romanian, you would also have heard Yiddish, Hebrew, German, French and, at one table for two, English. In spite of Stephen's multi-lingualism, we did not make much headway in bonding with our peers. The Israeli contingent behaved much as they did at home, and ignored our casual smiles, but nobody else seemed to want to engage with us either. As a rare Gentile at a Jewish event, it is the only time I have been made to feel less than welcome. It's an uncomfortable feeling, and one that many of the Festival's majority must have experienced for themselves.

None of that, possibly imagined, coolness could have detracted from the pleasure of performing in the National Theatre of Iasi; a spectacular Austrian confection from the end of the nineteenth century. An expertly painted ceiling, with a gigantic crystal chandelier, is ringed by three-dimensional plaster cherubs, so realistic that you expect one of them to fly down and poke you in the eye with a chubby toe. Only a couple of flaking damp patches and a certain shabbiness about the faded gold upholstery are witness to the financial struggle behind preserving this gem from Romania's most romantic age.

Our six-hour train journey back to Bucharest only took five. Timetables always err on the generous side so that trains are rarely late. Indeed, they sometimes stop in the middle of nowhere to idle some time away, then pull into the terminus dead on schedule.

Another week, another festival. This time the annual Caragiale International Theatre Festival, spread vibrantly throughout the city in theatres, converted warehouses, churches and restaurants. It was also where the International Association of Theatre Critics had chosen to have its annual jamboree. As with poachers and gamekeepers, the volatile relationship between actors and critics means that they rarely have anything to do with each other socially. That is difficult when you are the only performer amongst a party of English hacks at a British Council reception. In the event, it was a very good lunch, after which we all piled merrily into a minibus to take us to an afternoon of *Romeo and Juliet* in Hungarian. I found myself sandwiched between Irving Wardle, chief theatre critic in my youth at *The Times*, and Michael Billington, chief theatre critic in my youth, my maturity and my advancing middle age at *The Guardian*. I don't suppose Shakespeare in Hungarian held many surprises for him. The only shoptalk as we crawled through the back streets of Bucharest was a general consensus that the ideal length for a play was one-and-a-half hours. This *Romeo and Juliet* came in at just under four.

Afterwards, in dire need of sustenance, Stephen and I went in search of a restaurant that he remembered from the grim old days. Before the Second World War, it had apparently been a byword for excellence and sophistication, taking its cue, like so many things in that city, from Paris. By the sixties, when Stephen had first encountered it, its glory days were a faded memory, recalled only by the survival of some dusty chandeliers, but it had served as a cheap rendezvous for students and artists. So it was a pleasant surprise to find Casa Capsa still standing, its chandeliers intact. But now they sparkled in a setting that is one of the most elegant and beautifully run restaurants I have encountered anywhere.

The place was full and there seemed to be almost as many formally dressed waiters as there were diners. When we asked for the wine list, we were invited over to a table where every available bottle was standing for inspection, with a sommelier at hand. The food, though traditionally Eastern European in its emphasis on game and dark meat, was very French in its presentation, and utterly delicious. Three times during our meal, my huge and heavy table napkin slipped from my lap to the floor, and each time it was scooped up and discreetly replaced with a fresh one by one of the vigilant staff. This might have been intimidating, even embarrassing, but somehow everything was done without pretension and with a genuine conviction that this was what constituted good service.

It is how one imagines one's grandparents might have dined out, in the unlikely event that any of mine could have afforded it. Notions of elegance and service had been absent from this benighted capital for sixty-odd years, so the paradigm for excellence was from between the two world wars. We were in another time warp, but this time loving every minute of it.

Our performances behind us, we decided, on the last night, to pay a tribute to Mr Goldfaden by visiting the Jewish State Theatre which he had established in Bucharest as a successor to his company in Iasi. Nobody we asked en route seemed to know where it was, but eventually we found it in a very insalubrious quarter of the city, an isolated, rather dilapidated building in the middle of what looked like a bombsite. Inside, however, it was warm and welcoming, and we took our seats just as the curtain went up on a one-man show performed in Yiddish, and simultaneously translated into Romanian. But language was no barrier to its pleasures; based on the tales of Sholom Aleichem it was a witty and skilful evocation of life in the shtetl, a piece of nostalgia totally appropriate to its setting.

Just as Casa Capsa demonstrates an almost perverse resilience, so does this embattled little theatre. It was the first professional Jewish theatre company to be established anywhere in the world. It functions still, against many odds, not least the ever-diminishing number of Jews in Romania. From around a quarter of a million in 1900 the Jewish population has shrunk now to barely ten thousand people. Persecution and economic crises made mass emigration a major feature of the twentieth century, and Nazi persistence during the occupation depleted the numbers dramatically. After the war, the establishment of the state of Israel and the worsening living conditions under Ceausescu encouraged the majority of the remaining Jews to get out, and they still leave the country at the rate of four hundred a year.

But at the Jewish State Theatre, the show still goes on.

State of the Union

I thought Hull was the most depressing city in the world. But that was before I took *Shylock* to Middle America. I have played places that many New Yorkers don't even know exist, and if some of the names do ring a distant bell they blanch at the notion of someone actually having to go there. In fairness, the mention of New York, New York, in Clarkesville, Arkansas, provokes a similar reaction.

For every glamorous date I get in Santa Cruz, California, or Washington, DC, there will be a less appealing engagement in Muskegon, Michigan, or Greenville, Indiana. The fact that my touring schedule is usually at the tail end of autumn or just before spring probably colours my impression, which is of a greyish-brownish bleakness that could have been designed with Prozac in mind. Although thousands of miles apart, these places blur into one ghastly strip of fast-food restaurants, car concessionaries and cheap motels. The heart sinks on the drive from the nearest airport at the sterility of each characterless town.

Capricious perhaps best describes my feelings about the inhabitants; one day admiring, even envying them, and the next disapproving and despairing of them. Their generosity shames me, and their insularity shocks me. I always put on weight in the States, though I mostly can't find anything I really want to eat. I drink more than I do at home, though it's often hard to find someone to drink with.

I suppose being patronising towards Americans helps ease the pain of acknowledging their pre-eminence on the world stage. Americans might categorise that as envy, since they seem to genuinely believe that everyone in the world, given the choice, would choose to be American. Their self-image is of a fundamentally decent people and most of the ones I get to meet and work with are as welcoming, appreciative and eager to help as they believe themselves to be. But that doesn't mean I have to subscribe to their greatest myth: the quality of American service. Touring alone in the States, I have been exposed to some of the most insincere, unhelpful and downright inhospitable people I have encountered anywhere.

Take taxi drivers. Ever since that day I nearly killed John Fraser and myself in Nagadoches, Texas, a place to furrow a Manhattan brow if ever there was one, I do not drive in the USA. The only people not to drive in Middle America are prepubescent, senile or permanently inebriated. Not really qualifying on any of those counts, I, like Blanche Dubois, depend on the kindness of strangers. Or the local cab service.

Maybe because their clients are usually mewling and puking, incontinent or roaring drunk, taxi drivers are a suspicious breed. This suspicion either dictates that they will not turn up at all, or that if they do, they will be at least half-an-hour late and totally unrepentant. They will be enormously fat, and look as though they couldn't squeeze out of the driver's seat even if they wanted to, which they don't, especially if you have numerous and heavy bags. They behave as if your requiring their services is a strange aberration and the fact that you talk funny only confirms this. You have also obviously interrupted the continuous meals they eat in the confines of their vehicles, which are littered with McDonald's boxes, candy-bar wrappers and oozing sachets of tomato ketchup. They have no curiosity about you, the passenger, have no idea where you want to go and the fact that you don't know either because you are a stranger in town is merely another source of irritation. They also seem totally unaware that owing to their size and permanent occupation of their seat, the suspension in their cars is non-existent and that at your eventual destination, you will have several dislodged vertebrae and a permanent tilt to the left.

If the taxi has taken you to a hotel, the receptionist is quite likely to want your credit card details before making eye contact and, even then, the smile never quite reaches that far up the face. Most queries are greeted with dis-belief, as if your asking if the bar is still open after 9.30 p.m. is only proof of your being the sort of person who arrives by taxi. And yes, it isn't. 'Yes' is a word they have been trained to employ even when confirming a negative. 'Sorry' is a word they have been forbidden to use on pain of instant dismissal, and because nothing is ever their fault and, if it was, to admit it might make them liable to legal proceedings.

Most Middle Americans start eating dinner at about the same time that their English counterparts are finishing afternoon tea but, if you're lucky, the hotel restaurant may still be open. Now, French waiters can be rude, Spanish waiters haughty, Italian waiters overfamiliar, English waiters each of those things and slow to boot. But only American waiters think they are starring in a perpetual movie all about a witty, efficient, charismatic charmer. Alas, most of them are woefully miscast, their script is lousy, the dia-logue coach should be sacked, and the director should be forced to eat the food they serve.

Americans are very proud of their food. They prove this by making it an habitual topic of conversation and, of course, by consuming unimaginable amounts of it. Dining out on and around both seaboards you can eat very well, though not nearly as well as you are led to believe. What lies between is mostly a culinary wilderness. No further proof should be needed beyond the fact that the food of choice for most Middle Americans is Mexican cuisine – a contradiction in terms if ever there was one. How can a rolled up baby's diaper, including its contents, be called a cuisine? Why refry the beans? Why ruin an innocent piece of white fish with a bitter chocolate sauce? Why spoil the subtlety of a creamy avocado pear by mashing it up with a hot chilli pepper and watch it turn brown in front of your eyes? It must appeal to Americans because instead of settling for one flavour at a time, they can have all of them at once. Choice and choice in excess is a statement of freedom.

Bizarrely, what this variety confers is a sameness which at first you put down to faltering taste buds but is really the omnipresence of sugar. In a nation obsessed with low-fat and no-fat food, sugar seems to escape censure in the futile fight against obesity. The dozen or so dressings your saccharine waiter so proudly offers to pour over the taste-less and teeth-numbingly cold house salad all taste pri-marily of sugar. In a blind-tasting, the apple in the apple pie would not even register beyond it's primary ingre-dient, sugar.

The right to choose how you shorten your life through what you put in your mouth in America seems as enshrined as the freedom of speech. Unless, of course, it's a cigarette. I don't smoke cigarettes because, like President Clinton, I don't inhale. I smoke an occasional cigar. In America, I am a leper.

Now, I only attempt to light up out of a sense of mis-chief and because I know it teases. In public places, the reactions range from the aghast bartender – 'You're not going to *light* that, are you? – to the hysterical waitress who shouted across a diner, where I sat virtually alone in the small smoking section, 'Who done lit a pipe?' She waddled over to my table. 'You! Put that out. No pipes, no cee-gars! That is against the law!'

In parts of California, restaurants do not have a smoking section. After a meal, I once slunk out into the open air with my shameful half-corona and was pursued by a waiter who pointed to a notice forbidding smoking when standing still outside any public establishments in that part of the state, where your smoke might enter the premises through an open door or window. He moved me on. Within yards of where I stood, three huge air-conditioned coaches were parked, their engines running and fumes spewing from their exhausts.

You can smoke cigars in the company of other consenting adults in private, in specially designated Cigar Clubs and there is even a glossy magazine, *Cigar Aficionado*, for serious devotees who can drool over the prospect of forbidden Havanas, rather in the same way that I have seen Jewish friends salivate at the sight of a bacon sandwich.

Within the status of a private society, it is possible to find legitimacy for almost any activity in the States. Give your activity the status of a religion and you are protected by the American Constitution. A recent vice-presidential candidate pointed out that that constitution stipulates freedom of religion, not freedom from religion. A god is more or less mandatory. From the major faiths through to the most marginal cults, nearly all Americans believe in something, and are frankly suspicious of non-believers.

'How can you be so passionate in your play and say you don't believe in God?' an incredulous Catholic priest asked me just after I had 'come out' in front of an audience as an atheist. It was during a discussion panel at a community centre in Billings, Montana. They had booked *Shylock* to play the city theatre because of a recent event which had shone an unaccustomed media spotlight on the state capital. The event became known as 'The Christmas Menorahs'.

A Jewish family had put a lit menorah, the seven-headed Jewish candelabra, in their window in celebration of Hanukah, the Jewish festival which comes around at the same time as the Christian festival of Christmas. A stone was thrown through their window. In an inspired and moving retaliation to that act of hatred, the Jewish family's non-Jewish neighbours all put lit menorahs in their windows that Christmas.

The discussion panel after my performance included not only the incredulous priest but also the Jewish woman whose act of piety had provoked the incident. There was a Lutheran pastor too, who had enrolled as a member of the Hitler Youth in his native Nuremberg before the Second World War, and a cheerful, articulate woman who had spent three years of her childhood in a concentration camp. I was by far the least interesting person on the podium. But my confession of atheism was the one that provoked the most reaction. In America, I now call myself a humanist as that seems to cause less offence.

Beyond Belief

A friend of mine, who doesn't even have the excuse of being an American academic, has tried to convince me that Shakespeare was really a woman: Mary Sidney, poet and sister of Sir Philip, born in the same year as the other Shakespeare and outlasting him by five or six years. Then there are Marlowe's camp followers, the Baconites and the Earl of Oxford's champions, all with their claims to the true authorship. I don't lose much sleep fretting about who really wrote the plays but my instinct is that whoever it was was a theatre professional, writing for a troupe whose talents and shortcomings he knew intimately. Foremost among them, of course, was Richard Burbage.

Theatre anecdotes are as old as Thespis but one of the earliest English ones crops in the seventeenth-century diary of John Massingham:

> Upon a time when Burbage played Richard III, there was a citizen grew so far in liking him, that before she went from the play, she appointed him to come that night unto her by the name of Richard III. Shakespeare, overhearing their conclusion, went before, was entertained at his game ere Burbage came. The message being brought that Richard III was at the door, Shakespeare caused return to be made that William the Conqueror was before Richard III.

Whether or not they were rivals out of the workplace, their professional relationship must have been fascinating.

They were colleagues for over twenty years, and Burbage is known to have played all the great tragic roles, and maybe he even took over as Shylock once he realised what a cracking part it was. He was the more famous of the two men, owned most of the company shares and presumably had his own way in most things. The two men matured together. As Shakespeare grew wiser, wittier, more brilliant, it is fair to assume Burbage grew more skilful, more versatile, more accomplished. You don't have to be a scholar to observe how often Shakespeare will recycle good ideas, good relationships, even good lines. Many of those decisions might have been made in collaboration with, or even at the behest of Richard Burbage. Without diminishing the playwright's genius, isn't it possible that the phenomenon was at least partly a team effort?

But my pet theories would have cut no ice with Maurice Greenberg of Detroit, Michigan. Detroit makes Hull look positively inviting. The city centre is one of the most disturbing places I have ever been to, acres of urban wilderness where if people venture out at night, they do so only in locked cars. After race riots in the 1960s, 'the white flight' left metropolitan Detroit to a poor and mostly black population. Anyone who could afford it, moved to the suburbs, and I cannot deny that I was grateful to be living and performing in an affluent and boringly safe Jewish enclave where I was made to feel thoroughly welcome and where the crazy people were relatively harmless – like Maurice Greenberg.

Morrie told me that there are lines in *Love's Labour's Lost*, or maybe it was *Measure for Measure*, which are a direct translation from the Hebrew of lines in the Torah, the Jewish book of Law. This proves to Morrie that the complete works of Shakespeare were the joint labours of a group of Marranos, exiled Iberian Jews, living as Christians in London. The strange glint in Morrie's eye discouraged me from entering into a disputation with him, but he was delighted when I pointed out that the model on whom Shakespeare very likely based the character of Shylock was certainly a Marrano Jew.

Just a few years before *The Merchant* was written, there was a scandal involving Elizabeth I's personal physician, Roderigo Lopez. He was accused of a plot to poison the Queen, and was executed in front of a jeering crowd who mocked his protestations that he was a loyal Christian. His case inspired a wave of anti-Jewish feeling in the country, and the theatres cashed in by reviving several plays with Jewish characters. Marlowe's *The Jew of Malta* came back into the repertoire to boost the box office. Early in the play, Barabas, the eponymous role, gives us a brief resumé of his career to date:

> . . . I walk abroad a-nights,
> And kill sick people groaning under walls;
> Sometimes I go about and poison wells; . . .
> Being young, I studied physic, and began
> To practise first upon the Italian;
> There I enriched the priests with burials, . . .
> Then after that was I an usurer,
> And with extorting, cozening, forfeiting,
> And tricks belonging unto brokery,
> I filled the gaols with bankrouts in a year,
> And with young orphans planted hospitals . . .

Not surprisingly, the play is not often revived nowadays. But I did get to play Barabas in a rehearsed reading staged by Shakespeare's Globe on the South Bank. My favourite scene was where, in an attempt to murder my own daughter, I succeed in poisoning an entire nunnery. Outrageous stuff and a joy to play. But what was really evident from the reading is that the Christians and Muslims in the play are not much better people than is the Jew. His is just the best part. Marlowe after all was not interested in championing or rubbishing any particular religious group: he was an atheist. Maybe if he'd called himself a humanist, he wouldn't have come to such a sticky end.

Compared with Barabas, Shylock is a pussy-cat. Shakespeare made him Jewish because his audience loved to hate a Jew, as they had done since the Middle Ages.

*

As an adolescent, I remember answering the front door to two very tall, immaculately dressed young men with perfect teeth and shiny black shoes. In the Swansea of the 1960s, they looked impossibly glamorous, and when they asked in real American accents if they could talk to me about the state of the world, I was hugely flattered. It was raining, as it does most of the time in Swansea, and welcoming the distraction from my homework, I asked them in. They were about to cross the threshold when my father came down the stairs. Except on his two-week summer holiday, when he wore his Armstrong-tartan tie or very occasionally an open-necked shirt, my father always wore his clerical collar. One look at him and the young Adonises' enthusiasm to come in and refuse a cup of tea melted away. Dad was very polite but gave them pretty short shrift. I had missed my chance to learn about Mormonism – and to save my soul.

Years later, there was a scandal in the little Sussex town of East Grinstead, where the Mormon Church has its British headquarters. A young Mormon claimed he had been tied to the bottom of his bed and raped by a rapacious female. In those politically incorrect days, there was no sympathy for either party, just much speculation about who did what to whom and how. The details and the outcome of the case I have quite forgotten, except the ribald references made to the young man's Mormon-designated underwear, which the gossip implied was designed to restrict rather than encourage access.

That was the sum total of my exposure to the Church of Jesus Christ of Latter-day Saints when I arrived in the Promised Land. Robert Friedman and I were both surprised to get a booking to perform at Brigham Young University, Salt Lake City, Utah, but it fitted well into the tour and the presenter there was very enthusiastic after seeing us showcase the play in New York.

Len Crutchley was indeed wearing a suit, shiny black shoes and a big smile when he met me at the airport, but the talk en route to my hotel was entirely secular. Apart from the Book of Mormon placed alongside the Gideon Bible in the bedside drawer and the absence of the familiar coffee-making machine by the sink, the hotel might have been in any mid-West town. Forewarned, I had brought a kettle and my own supplies of coffee and other restricted substances, but, as so often, I had overreacted.

Len drove me out of town to a vast supermarket to stock up on supplies of whatever I might need during the week's residency, and pointed out the six-packs of locally brewed ale, which he assured me, though not from personal experience, was very well thought of. He was an extraordinarily attentive and patient host over the coming days. In his forties, married with half-a-dozen children, and evidently prominent in his local church, he answered all the questions I felt it appropriate to ask him, in a soft, modulated voice, with an old-fashioned and very careful vocabulary. Desperate to know why he had booked *Shylock*, I started asking him about how he chose his theatre season.

'It's not easy, Gareth,' he admitted. 'You see, I am very restricted in what I can present in our facility, Gareth.' Len used my name at least once in every sentence as if he were afraid that by not repeating it constantly, he might forget it entirely. 'There are certain rules, Gareth. Onstage, there must be no smoking, no drinking, no nudity, no foul language and . . . ' – he paused quite theatrically – ' . . . no lewdness, Gareth'.

Innocent on all counts, I thought, but who else would qualify?

'Our last visitors were an excellent troupe of disabled acrobats from China, Gareth. I wish you could have seen them.'

So did I.

Hardly any contemporary theatre would pass Len's strict criteria, so I could see the attraction of the classics. But why a play about Shakespeare's Jew which is frankly critical of both the Christian hypocrisy in *The Merchant of Venice* and the Gentile propaganda of the New Testament? Mormons, it transpires, do not consider themselves to be Gentiles.

Len told me a story about the first non-Mormon to run for the office of Governor of the state of Utah. During his campaign in 1916, Simon Bamberger visited a remote community which had been settled by Norwegian converts to Mormonism. When his train drew into the station, he was confronted by a mountain of a man who told him he might just as well go straight back where he had come from because no 'damned Gentile' was going to be allowed to make a speech in their meeting house. Bamberger replied that as a Jew he had been called many a bad name in his time but never a 'damned Gentile'. Len, at the most animated I ever saw him, launched into his well-rehearsed impersonation of the Norwegian's response:

' "You, a Yew, an Israelite. Hear him men, hear him, he's not a Yentile, he's a Yew, an Israelite. Velcome my friend! Velcome, our next Governor!" And do you know, Gareth, he was right; Simon Bamberger won the election. And he was not only a Jew, he was a Democrat.'

The Mormon empathy with Jews and Judaism is as old as the religion itself. According to Mormon belief, American Indians are all descended from three groups of immigrants who were led from their original homes in the Near East to America.

Joseph Smith, the founder of Mormonism, claimed to have unearthed tablets of gold on a hillside in western New York and to have been told by an angel that it was the story of these ancient peoples written in an Egyptian dialect. With the help of the angel, the spirit of God and a pair of sacred spectacles, he translated the golden plates. The Book of Mormon I found in my bedside table was the result.

I did try to read it but, to a non-believer like me, it came across like a clever but very tedious pastiche of the Old Testament. It is full of battles fought by people with names that sound like non-prescription drugs such as Lamoni and Amulek. I never got as far as the most important bit where Jesus Christ visited America after his crucifixion to minister to the inhabitants, but the Mormons' Jewish origins are evidently fundamental to the scripture. And Jewish metaphor is not just in the ancient history. Smith proclaimed, 'We believe in the literal gathering of Israel and in the restoration of the Ten Tribes; that Zion will be built upon this continent.' The journey of the early Mormons across the States in the nineteenth century and the persecutions that dogged their odyssey have obvious parallels in the history of the Hebrews. To Mormons, the Utah desert was a latter-day Zion, and the Great Salt Lake a latter-day Dead Sea. So a play where major themes are anti-Semitism and the consequence of religious intolerance was not such an unlikely choice after all.

The three young technicians assigned to help me stage the show were still undergraduates at Brigham Young University. I do not know which surprised me more, their professionalism or their maturity. Brian, Eric and David had each just returned from two years of missionary work overseas. Like the couple who doorstepped me in Swansea all those years before, they had been sent abroad in their late teens to convert the heathen. Whatever I think about their beliefs and their lifestyle, I could never deny their courage and their commitment.

In any given year, there are around sixty thousand Mormons serving as full-time missionaries in about one hundred and twenty countries worldwide. They train for ten weeks, studying doctrine, learning to teach the gospel and acquiring essential communication skills. Presumably they also carry large quantities of shoe polish and toothpaste. Part of the process is learning the language of whatever country you are called to serve in. The former Soviet countries, where religious practices were discouraged for so long, are fertile territory for sects like the Mormons. Brian had served in Russia and was fluent in Russian. Eric had been sent to Romania and managed to master that language and a smattering of Hungarian too. And the missionaries are not featherbedded; they live their lives among whatever community they are assigned to and tolerate the same conditions. So it was David who really had my sympathy. He had served his two years in Hull.

I did not ask them what their relative success rates had been, but I did learn that conversions to Mormonism are not limited to the living. It is a religious obligation on Mormons to track down their deceased forebears and baptise them in sacred ceremonies where living members of the Church assume their names. Joseph Smith, their founder, warned them that failure to do so was 'at the peril of their own salvation'. Being baptised is the first step towards that salvation and entry to the Mormon heaven, known as the Celestial Kingdom. Hitler and Anne Frank were both admitted to the Celestial Kingdom, which surprised me greatly, though probably not as much as it must have surprised them. Along with Albert Einstein, Sigmund Freud, David Ben-Gurion, Golda Meir and Menachem Begin, they were posthumously baptised by proxy into the Church of Jesus Christ of the Latter-day Saints.

But it's not only prominent Jews who have been offered the chance of salvation. Names from amongst the millions who perished during the Holocaust were also researched and given baptism with no reference to their surviving families or the sensibilities of other Jews, who had to point out that as the victims had not chosen to convert during their lives, it was beyond ethical bounds to do so on their behalf after their deaths. Only in 2001 did the Mormon Church give in to pressure and remove many of the names from their records.

Genealogy is big business in Utah. The Family History Library, pointed out to me with great pride just across the road from the main Mormon temple in Salt Lake City, houses the biggest genealogical database in the world. Unless, after my visit, they have decided that I am beyond saving, I may well be in there somewhere. So may you.

There may be black students at Brigham Young University but I did not see any. Being black was known in the Mormon Church as 'The Curse of Cain' and until 1978 no one of the black race was entitled to hold God's priesthood. It may have rethought its racial policy, but the church still has its blind spots. Any Mormon who admits to being homosexual will be pressured to abandon this 'evil' aspect of his nature. A refusal to remain celibate could result in excommunication.

In time, the Mormon Church may well move the goalposts again. But will they ever conclude, as I have, that their religion is based on an elaborate con trick by a brilliant charlatan? If they do, then I hope for the sake of the devout, kind and sincere people I met in Utah that it's a gentle revelation.

Shylock Wallah

'It's a-like a fuckin' circus!' my Italian friend Luca cried at the end of his first day in India. That morning I had collected him from Delhi airport, and we'd driven in air-conditioned comfort along the dual carriageways that led to our five-star hotel. After lunch I had had to go off to rehearsals, and when I got back Luca was in his room, looking grey and shocked. He had decided to take a walk by himself to see the Red Fort and been totally unprepared for what he encountered. After likening it to one of Dante's circles of Hell, he hit on the circus metaphor: 'And I hate the fuckin' circus!'

I'm not that keen on the circus either, but I love India, and as Luca and I share so many tastes and opinions, I was intrigued to find out why he evidently didn't. Principally, for me, it's the historical associations, the centuries of mutual friendship and hostility. Whether it be family connections or the media-fed nostalgia for the Raj or the presence of so many people from the subcontinent in British cities, there is a bond of familiarity between the two peoples that would be a mystery to an Italian. With little of an imperial legacy, modern Italy has been spared the guilt and the consequences of empire.

Then there is the cuisine. Luca looks at first uncomprehending and then pitying when you explain that the national dish of the United Kingdom is something called Chicken Tikka Marsala.

But the real glue that bonds the Anglo-Indian relationship is the English language. The Parliaments of both nations conduct their business in English, and any Indian fortunate enough to experience secondary education will have been exposed not only to English language but also to English literature. They will almost certainly have encountered at least one of Shakespeare's plays. And not in the abbreviated form that seems to pass for the teaching of Shakespeare now in many British schools, but the whole play in all its complex entirety.

Often the first and most frequently taught play in Indian schools is *The Merchant of Venice*. It may seem an odd favourite, but it has those same virtues that used to recommend it to a syllabus in Britain; there is more romance than sex, and not too much bawdy. There are moral allegories, and the ostensible defeat of bloodthirsty revenge by righteous justice and mercy. I lost count of the number of people who could give flawless renditions of Portia's 'quality of mercy' speech. In fact, it was astonishing how many folk, from clerks and hotel receptionists to computer whizz kids, can quote speeches from Shakespeare, often at dizzying length. If you pick up any of the excellent English language newspapers in India, you can be sure that the front page will have at least one quotation from Shakespeare, probably not attributed but nonetheless authentic. So to perform in India, you need to have total mastery of the text. But they want and expect a lot more than mere competence. Indian audiences are very discerning, which is a polite way of saying that they are very hard to please.

I had toured the subcontinent with Fanny in the early 1980s, when we had played Bangladesh, India and Sri Lanka in a whistle-stop couple of weeks. I had experienced those mixed reactions of wonder and disgust that everyone must surely feel on first confronting that maelstrom of humanity, so I was prepared for most of the assaults that India would make on all my senses and on my sensibilities too.

Twenty years had seen the arrival of a new International Airport in Delhi, a sparkling new metro system in Calcutta, the sprouting of the once-banned Coca-Cola signs everywhere and a very obvious diminution of the Gandhian ideals that had made the country such a beacon amongst the newer democracies.

On that earlier tour we had roughed it a bit, but this time the tour was sponsored by the Oberoi group of hotels, one of the most luxurious in the world. Our suites were vast, with acres of bathroom where your shower suite doubled as a private steam bath. A bell by the bed summoned your personal butler to cater to any whim, and when room service arrived, it looked so beautiful you were reluctant to spoil its silver symmetry. Every one of the staff from receptionists to lift attendants and waiters seemed to know you by name including the seven-foot-tall Pathan warrior gentleman with the magnificent waxed whiskers and spotless white gloves, who saluted crisply before springing to open the door of your brand new Range Rover.

A hundred yards of immaculately maintained driveway, bordered by rose beds and scented by jasmine, led out through forbidding security gates onto the city streets. And there was the real India, the inescapable India. The India that Luca had unwittingly stepped into on his first day.

The process worked in reverse too, as when you picked your way over the emaciated and ragged bodies at the bedlam of a city railway station, and ignored the relentless hawkers and the beggars as you stepped up into the cool and calm of the first-class carriages of the Shatabdi Express for a pampered journey across the burning plains.

But the realities of life are not so easily ignored from the carriage window unless you avert your gaze or draw the curtains. Most such long rail journeys begin just after dawn and the first hour or so of the journey is a sluggish progress through the suburban slums that encroach on every major Indian metropolis. Early rising was an un-welcome novelty to me, but the first glimpse of daylight is the signal for the daily Indian routine to begin, which of course includes attending to natural functions. Every hun-dred yards or so there is a squatting male figure nonchal-antly taking a shit in whatever patch of grass or scrub he reaches when nature calls. He seems totally unaware that hundreds of people can see him about his business and when the train comes to a halt right by his exposed form, there is no sense that he feels any invasion of his privacy. His face maintains a look of contemplative contentment at this one moment of the day when he can be alone with his thoughts and his moving bowels.

Our first train journey was six hours south from Delhi to the city of Ajmer. Ajmer is nothing to get too excited about, unless you're a Muslim pilgrim, in which case you make a beeline for the Daragh, tomb of the founder of the Sufi order of Chishti and one of the holiest Islamic shrines in India. In fact, if you make seven beelines to the Daragh, it is the dervish equivalent of one visit to Mecca.

The British Council had arranged for us to perform for the students of Mayo College. After a nondescript drive out of town from the station, you reach the rural outskirts and through the clouds of dust thrown up by your vehicle emerges an extraordinarily imposing building, all turrets and minarets. Built in the Indo-Saracenic style, whatever that is, it looks for all the world like a fairy tale Maharaja's palace. And, indeed, the first pupil of Mayo College in 1875 was a Maharaja, Mangal Sing of Alwar.

After the Indian Mutiny, the nervous Brits realised that winning the hearts and minds of India's traditional rulers was essential if the Raj was to survive. And the most efficient way was to educate the young elite and create what Macaulay called a 'class of people – Indian in Blood and Colour, but English in opinions, in morals and in Intellect'. At an annual prize-giving a few years after its foundation, the Viceroy, Lord Lytton, declared: 'This college is India's Eton and you are India's Eton boys.' I suppose the pupils were meant to be flattered. But some of the stories, real or apocryphal, about Mayo's illustrious old boys make most of Eton's alumni look like rejects from an inner-city comprehensive. They arrived on the first day of term with dozens of elephants, polo ponies, livestock and scores of servants. One Maharaja's son was allowed only to wash in the holy waters of the Ganges, so caravans were regularly despatched from his home state, hundreds of miles away, bearing his bath water.

A royal lineage is not essential to get you into Mayo College nowadays, just money. And some fifteen years ago the school made a decision which would have launched the Viceroy on his very own mutiny. Mayo started admitting girls. Their premises are a respectful half a mile away from the imposing boys' school and their campus is built in a utilitarian 1980s style with not a minaret to be seen. Alas, our performance was in their huge and echoing school hall with the boys marched down the road just minutes before the play began.

Unfortunately, just after I started the show, a teacher must have decided that the heat being generated by this adolescent mélange was too much and switched on every wall and ceiling fan in the building. The racket was so loud that, though we all stayed cool, I doubt if the audience heard one word in three and I was hoarse with shouting by the curtain call.

Afterwards, the boys having been despatched back to their dorms, we were bidden to a teetotal reception, hosted by the imperious and impressive headmistress, Mrs Jamila Singh. Everything was done with wonderfully old-fashioned courtesy, as I imagine it might have been at Roedean between the wars, except that all the teachers were wearing saris. After speeches of welcome and speeches of thanks, exchanging of gifts and endless acknowledgements, the girls were let loose on the visitors to practise their social skills, though none of them, it has to be said, needed much practice. They were the most polite, articulate and cultured young people I have ever met, and if some of them lacked a European girl's self-confidence, they were all the more charming for that. I got into conversation with a stunningly beautiful girl from Simla in the north, where her father was obviously a prominent and presumably rich politician. As we chatted, the servants were doing the rounds with plates of vegetarian savouries, which I adore. There were bhajis and pakoras and something delicious served with a tamarind sauce, which the server told me were called bhel puris. I asked my new friend what they were made of. There was a moment of slight embarrassment: 'I am so sorry,' she said very sweetly, 'I have no idea. I do not go into the kitchen. The ingredients of that tit-bit are as much of a magical mystery tour to me as they are to you.'

*

There was some doubt about whether one of our dates might have to be cancelled. I was reminded of the tour to Israel where Jerusalem became out of bounds for political reasons. A few months before I left London, there had been an incident horribly reminiscent of the atrocities that followed the partition of India at independence. A train load of Hindu pilgrims were returning from a religious pilgrimage to Ahmedabad in the state of Gujarat. The train was allegedly halted by disaffected Muslims who massacred the passengers. Reprisals, of course, followed. There are conflicting versions of the story but the resultant bloodshed was real enough.

When we reached Ahmedabad, things had calmed down for the time being, but there was disturbing evidence of the recent violence. On our way from the airport, we passed the burnt-out shell of a hotel that had been run for decades without incident by a Muslim family, but which had fallen foul of the Hindu revenge attack. The family had fled Gujarat.

It's a potent irony that Ahmedabad is home to the Gandhi Ashram, a very tranquil settlement on the banks of the sluggish river Sabarhati that runs through the city. It was set up in 1920 and became the centre of the Indian Freedom Movement. From here, Gandhi began his famous 'Dandi March' to the sea in protest at the tax imposed on salt by the British Government. His emphases on peaceful protest and religious harmony seem even more pertinent today. I couldn't help thinking, as I walked around his sparse bungalow, that if he hadn't been cremated on the banks of the sacred Ganges, the current situation in Gujarat would have had him spinning in his grave.

Pieces of the cotton cloth the Mahatma wove and some of his very few possessions are exhibited. There are quotations from his writings and extracts from his speeches displayed above photographs of him with the good and the great of the twentieth century, and one very touching image of him talking and laughing with the women mill workers of Lancashire whom he was trying to put out of work in the name of justice for Indian cotton workers.

Walking away from the Ashram in the pink glow of the late afternoon, I found myself caught up in a boisterous street celebration of Ganesh, the elephant-headed Hindu deity. He is arguably the most loved of all their gods and images of him are everywhere in India. They are often quite playful, and I even saw one of him with a pipe in his mouth and a bottle of Guinness in his pocket. (At least it wasn't Coca-Cola.) Here, Ganesh was mounted on a bullock cart, festooned with flowers and surrounded by gifts of fruit and sweetmeats. The crowd was about fifty strong, their faces smeared with multi-coloured powders, and they were perfectly happy for me to join in their progress down to the river where the portly old jumbo was tipped into the water. Amidst much cheering, he bobbed off slowly downstream, shedding his garlands as he went. Only as the people started to disperse and stumble away was I aware how drunk, or high, some of them were, the result of a full day of celebration, and I hoped that the local Muslim population would have the sense to keep well out of their way in the falling darkness.

Most of our hosts who worked for the British Council were Hindu by birth, but, like so many non-practising Jews, they were fiercely secular. Rajiv, a slight, pale and very cultivated young man, was deputed to look after us on our visit to Rajasthan, but he was less than enthusiastic when Stephen, my tour manager again on that trip, and I asked to be taken to visit the temples at Pushkar. It is one of the holiest Hindu sites in India, but Rajiv had never been and claimed not even to know the legend of how it came into being. We had read the guidebook so we told him: The Lord Brahma, the Creator, dropped lotus flowers from his hand to fall to earth and kill a demon. Where three of the petals landed, small blue lakes were formed in the middle of the desert, and it was here that the Lord Brahma convened a gathering of the entire Hindu pantheon of some nine hundred thousand celestial beings.

The water of the lakes is believed to cleanse the soul of all impurities. Rajiv didn't seem very impressed.

As there are five hundred temples in and around Push-kar, he prevailed on us to visit only one, the only temple in India dedicated to the Lord Brahma. We removed our shoes at the entrance and fought our barefoot way through the dense and noisily devout throng towards the four-headed image of Brahma, raised on a platform in the middle of the courtyard. Our progress was made even slower by the presence of dozens of holy but mischievous monkeys and by their excrement, which found its way ineluctably between our toes. Rajiv seemed to be hating every minute of it, so we cut our visit short to go down to the lakeside and buy offerings for the gods to float upon the waters. The guides, of course, saw us coming and started an interminable ceremony which ended up with us strewing petals on the lake and repeating incomprehensible prayers before paying handsomely for the privilege. Rajiv stood aloof and was obviously mystified by the delight we took in the wonderful chaos of it all.

*

Nearly everyone I spoke to in India who had studied *The Merchant* and had also been to see my play was surprised at my revisionist view of Shylock and my emphasis on his Jewishness. To them, it had always been a tale of good and evil, virtuous heroes and a rapacious villain. In a nation where the proportion of Christians is relatively small and the number of Jews almost negligible, the religious allegiances of the characters are there just to add colour and texture.

With the proselytising of the Empire, and the omni-presence of Western influences, Indians could not but be familiar with Christian symbols and imagery, but I had no idea whether Jews had made any impact on the sub-continent. In Mumbai (Bombay), I found some small legacy of British Jewry in landmarks like the Jacob Circle and the Flora Fountain which memorialise the Sassoon family, but I doubt if many Indians are aware of their pro-venance. In the other twelve cities of the tour, my researches were even more fruitless. Then, in the steamy south-western port of Cochin, in Kerala, I found a place called Jew Town.

How Jews reached the coast of Kerala is a matter of much romantic speculation. Did they arrive in King Solomon's merchant fleet, or were they the descendants of the slaves taken to Babylon by King Nebuchadnezzar? What isn't disputed is that from the fifth to the fifteenth century there was a virtually independent principality there, ruled over by a Jewish Prince.

It was after a murderous onslaught on the community by the Moors in the sixteenth century that the Jews built their town in Cochin and, in 1568, the synagogue, which still stands today. More persecution followed by the Portuguese colonisers, and it was only under the later Dutch and British rulers that the Jewish enclave thrived once more.

It was the foundation of Israel which spelt the beginning of the end for Kerala's Jews, but Indians remain proud that the Jews in their midst left, not because of intolerance or discrimination but in order to return to their Promised Land.

Jew Town is a narrow street lined with cluttered little shops, no longer run by Jews but by traders from Kashmir, with whom they share a reputation for shrewd business practices. On the left-hand side at the end of the street is an archway that leads into the precincts of the synagogue. The temple itself, surrounded by ancient gravestones, is a cool, almost austere building. Apart from the floor, covered with blue and white Dutch tiles, and the centrally placed pulpit, it reminded me of the simple chapels of my Presbyterian childhood. Before we left, I struck up a conversation with the lady in charge of the monument. She was, she told me, from one the last six remaining Jewish families in the state of Kerala.

A few days later, I met another Jewess, but the community she came from is happily far from endangered. Jill Singer, born in New York, now lives in Auroville, a utopian community just outside the old French possession of Pondicherry in Tamil Nadu.

It was just like the British Council's arts manager in south India, Rathi Jafer, to arrange a performance at such an unlikely location. Rathi is one of those rare administrators who has mastered all the management disciplines, but can still infuse her work with originality and flair.

From Chennai (Madras) we drove south, stopping, over a lunch of king prawns and fresh mango, to gaze at the sparkling waters of the Coromandel Coast. The approach to Auroville is surprisingly low-key, a potholed road lined with food stalls and bicycle-hire shops. But quite soon, the landscape surprises you by its lush greenery, and, even more so, by its orderliness. Given that thirty years ago these acres were designated barren, the achievement of the Aurovillians is all the more remarkable. With their New Age credentials, it comes as no surprise that they have made the desert bloom using only natural energy, generated by solar panels and windmills.

Founded in 1968, Auroville was conceived as 'The City of Dawn', a community with a spiritual ideal which owes nothing to any particular faith. The members aim to achieve harmony by hard physical work and spiritual discipline. There are few rules, but within the commune the consumption of alcohol by its members is not allowed. So I was jolly glad we had brought our own.

Tapas Bhatt, who co-ordinates the arts programme at Auroville, was a passionate advocate for her adopted home and an authoritative guide. In her wit, enthusiasm and readiness to admit the fallibility of the whole social experiment, she was almost persuasive. She took us to look at thriving organic farms and model communities within the settlement with names like 'Certitude', 'Sincerity' and 'Revelation'. There was a huge variety of architectural styles, and the dwellings ranged from modest apartments to very stylish houses in their own grounds. Within the notion of communal ownership, there is evidently a recognition that some are more equal than others.

The highlight of the tour was a visit to the Matri Mandir or 'dwelling place of The Mother'. It was The Mother who from her ashram in nearby Pondicherry conceived of Auroville, and the 'City of Dawn' is the embodiment of her philosophy. I read a book of edited highlights of her pronouncements; they struck me as mostly unremarkable, naive, even banal. The Matri Mandir she described as 'a symbol of the Divine's answer to man's inspiration for perfection'. It is a vast, gold-plated globe, thirty-six metres in diameter, and although it was begun in 1970, is still years away from completion. As honoured guests, we were allowed to approach the edifice along a pathway that led under a beautiful and vast banyan tree, where we were encouraged to pause and meditate. Day-trippers, who are allowed to visit the sight, have to queue up, often for hours, and file into the structure in total silence. The inside of the globe resembles a space-age building site, partly clad in white marble, but mostly covered in enormous dust sheets. The pilgrimage climaxes with an ascent into a totally white room and a brief glimpse of the crystal ball, reputedly the largest in the world, which rests in a golden cradle at its centre. You then have to slowly retrace your steps, and hope that your cynicism is not written too large on your features. To my spiritual antennae, the whole thing struck me as the grossest folly. But I daresay there are people who think that about Chartres Cathedral.

*

Our last performance in India could have been an anti-climax. After the dynamism of Bangalore, the chaos of Calcutta, and the awesome beauty of Jaipur, we ended up in Coimbatore, the garment capital of Tamil Nadu and proudly claimed to be 'the Manchester of India'. A visit from a touring show like mine was very rare, and we played to a highly expectant full house. Many of the audience belonged to an organisation called British Scholars Abroad, men and women educated in the UK and now practising law or medicine or business management in this prosperous city. At a smart reception afterwards, I was basking in the adulation of my cultured and appreciative audience. A short dark-suited man approached me, beaming. 'Thank you. Thank you.' He took my hand and shook it fervently.

'We so love our Shakespeare in India. His wisdom, his poetry, his wit.' Modestly taking the credit on behalf of my co-author, I assured him what a pleasure it had been to perform in his city. 'And tell me,' he said, still holding on to my hand. 'How well are you acquainted with *The Maha-bharata*?' The honest answer was hardly at all. I bluffed a little, admitting to know that it was an epic Sanskrit poem, full of fabulous tales of gods and dynastic struggles, and that Peter Brook had directed a very long play from bits of it. 'But you have never read any of it in translation?'

I hadn't. His smile faded slightly, and he loosened his grip on my hand.

'That is such a shame. You come to India and bring us the wonderful gift of your greatest poet, whom we love and revere in equal measure. And yet, you know almost nothing about the foremost source of our classical civilisation. The sharing of cultures between two great traditions should really not be a one-way process, Mr Armstrong. May I suggest that when you visit us again, which I earnestly hope will be soon, you come a little better prepared.' The smile reappeared and he drifted off, leaving me firmly in my place.

The Mahabharata is the longest poem in world literature: I read somewhere that it is fifteen times longer than the Bible. Next day, with a hugely condensed paperback version weighing down my luggage, Stephen and I set off for some rest and recreation. The great advantage of finishing our tour in Coimbatore is that city's proximity to the Nilgiri Hills, and the 'Queen of Hill Stations', Ootacamund. In the time of the Raj, it had been the most popular hill retreat in peninsular India, and it was where the British inhabitants who chose to 'stay on' after independence, ended their days. In spite of the dwindling worth of their tiny pensions, the Brits struggled to keep up their old lifestyle, and retained their notorious snobbishness. Even now, the town is referred to as 'Snooty Ooty'.

Apart from a kind climate and a splendid botanical garden, originally laid out by gardeners sent from Kew in the mid-nineteenth century, we were rather disappointed with Ooty. The wise and thoughtful Rathi had advised us to stop over in nearby Coonoor, and we fell under its tranquil spell immediately. Arriving at a compound of neat, well-spaced bungalows, we were greeted with pots of orange pekoe tea, served on the immaculate lawns. In the evening, whilst we feasted in the dark wood-panelled dining room, a fire was being lit in the grate of our sitting room to take the chill off the crisp night air.

But the pleasures of getting to, and staying in the hills were as nothing compared to the joy of coming back down again. The Nilgiri Blue Mountain Railway has one of the last functioning steam routes in South Asia. The distance is less than thirty kilometres from Coonoor to the lowland town of Mettupalayam, and the journey takes four bone-shaking hours. The train often moves no faster than walking pace, but that is fast enough when the scenery is as spectacular as it is over the Hulikal ravine. The perilous bridges, the pitch-black tunnels, and the vertiginous descents make it the most exhilarating journey I have ever taken. Our train was monumentally late reaching Mettu-palayam, which meant that darkness had already fallen as we pulled into the town. On the low brick walls of the houses that lined the track, parents lifted their delighted children shoulder-high so that they could try and catch the bright red sparks that flew from our engine. For those few minutes, I clung to the illusion that everyone in the world felt as happy as I did.

On the sluggish road journey to the airport next day, our progress was made even slower by the huge open lorries that hogged the road in the opposite direction. Their cargo consisted of three or four men pressed against the wooden sides of the vehicle to make room for its main occupant, a huge working elephant. Sometimes the lorries would pull over, and the mahouts would slosh buckets of water over their charges to keep them cool. As a reciprocal gesture, the elephants would occasionally relieve them-selves, and temporarily lay the dust with the torrent of their micturition. The mystery of their journey was solved by *The Hindu* newspaper next day. Headlined 'Elephants get into vehicles without fuss', it continued:

> The month-long rest and restoration camp for elephants from different parts of the state ended yesterday. Rest stations providing water, medical and other facilities were set up on the route and even weak elephants such as Vijayalaksh of Ramananthapram could withstand the trip.
>
> Some mahouts took extra care to prevent their animals getting irritated during the journey, as they could be experiencing a 'holiday hangover'. Children queued up along the route to offer the animals fruits and wish them 'bon voyage'.

India. Truly, a glorious fucking circus.

Bloody Justice

Most of the graves were bordered with low rectangular fences of wrought iron. It made them look like so many half-submerged bedsteads, an impression reinforced by the snow lying thick on the ground, providing a pristine white duvet. The poorer graves were just marked with sawn-off scaffolding poles crudely welded together in the shape of crosses, and only a few had stone or marble headstones.

The grave I had been looking for was altogether more imposing: a tall eight-sided wooden cross of the Orthodox Church, painted glossy brown with a brass plaque nailed at its centre and, nestling in the snow at its foot, three or four bunches of tiny white flowers in tight bud. On nearby graves, any floral tributes were crude plastic imitations, but these looked fresh. They were snowdrops, their stems bound with wire and covered in thick green leaves to make a compact, respectful posy.

The graveyard was in Kiev, capital of Ukraine, close to the infamous site of the Baba Yar massacre where thirty thousand people, mostly Jews, had been slaughtered and tipped into mass graves by the Nazi occupiers. The grave was that of a thirteen-year-old child, Andrey Yustshinsky, who had died thirty years before Baba Yar. But somebody had remembered him sufficiently to bring fresh flowers there in a bitterly cold winter.

Andrey should have been at school on 12 March 1911, but he never appeared. A week later he was found in a cave. He was in a sitting position with his hands tied behind his back. He was naked except for his underwear, and his body bore forty-seven stab wounds. At his funeral, leaflets were distributed alleging that he was the victim of a blood sacrifice. Six months later, the Jewish foreman of a local brickworks, Mendel Beilis, was accused of ritual murder. His trial was the last recorded legal case relating to the 'blood libel'.

In *Shylock*, I re-enact the first recorded case, the death of little William of Norwich in 1144. In 1911, the year in which my mother was born, the calumny still had sufficient credence for the Beilis case to come to court. The nationalist Czarist faction were virulently anti-Semitic and wanted to exploit the child's death for propaganda purposes. In spite of their hand-picking a judge and jury, spying on the jury's deliberations and withholding documents and evidence which would have proved him innocent, Beilis was acquitted. A silent crowd, waiting outside the courthouse for the result, erupted into cheering when the 'not guilty' verdict was announced. A blatant injustice that would have shamed the whole nation had been averted. Beilis emigrated first to Palestine and later to America, where his daughter Rae Beilis, now in her nineties, still lives in New York.

*

'And are there any Jewish students here?' No hands went up. I had asked the question quite casually during a post-performance question-and-answer session in Gorlovka at the Institute of Foreign Languages where Ukraine's brightest and best learn English, French and German to use in careers in education and diplomacy. Later, their professor told me that there were probably a couple of dozen Jewish youngsters in the group of around three hundred but that none of them would have been prepared to draw attention to themselves by admitting it. He insisted that there was no blatant anti-Semitism but that the legacy of the past was difficult to erase even for the new post-Soviet generation of Ukrainian Jews.

This reluctance to 'come out' as Jewish is not peculiar to Eastern Europe. Many of the most fiercely active men and women in Jewish life that I encounter in England and the States are the children of parents who denied their Jewishness altogether or chose to make it peripheral to their lives. I wouldn't presume to know whether that generation was motivated by indifference, fear, or the guilt of being survivors of attempted genocide, but the vehemence of their offspring in asserting their religious and cultural identity is an obvious reaction to the imminent loss of their heritage.

Much of the impetus for reviving and restoring Jewish life in Ukraine comes from the New World. Yaakov Bleich, a wise and witty man from Brooklyn, New York, is Ukraine's Chief Rabbi. After a performance, he gave me useful notes about the pronunciation of some of the Yiddish words I use in the show. It is, he told me, still the language of the hearth for most of his elderly parishioners, and the language he chooses to converse in with his own young family.

As well as performing in Kiev to crowds of over eight hundred people, we travelled on a slow overnight train to the industrial town of Donetsk in the south-east of the country, not far from the Russian border. The train is patrolled by uniformed female officials with a zeal reminiscent of a previous era, and they take no account of a westerner's expectation of privacy, throwing open compartment doors unannounced to prepare you for a station stop or to thrust a hot glass of morning tea into the hand which isn't clutching a snatched pillow over private parts.

The only way to get to sleep in the cramped, airtight

compartments is to drink lots of the local honey and red pepper vodka, chasing each glass with a vinegary gherkin or a slice of pig fat eaten *au naturel*. The vodka certainly makes the tracks feel smoother and the narrow bunk beds less lumpy, and miraculously leaves you with no trace of a hangover. The locals use it too, to combat the fearsome cold, which during our trip was hovering around minus twenty degrees centigrade, and made worse by the biting winds whistling off the Steppes. Drunk in the traditional manner in a single gulp, rather than with genteel sips, its anaesthetic properties are undeniable.

Driving from the station to our hotel, we passed a huge statue of Lenin which the town council had evidently decided not to demolish. We also passed Mr Hughes from the coal mines of South Wales, who is credited with founding the city of Donetsk in the nineteenth century and who is honoured with a somewhat smaller statue. Donetsk is twinned with Sheffield but the honour should clearly have gone to Merthyr Tydfil.

Coal mining and steel works apart, Ukraine has other things in common with Wales. Dominated for centuries by a bigger, bullying neighbour, the survival of the indigenous language has become a vital cultural issue. We were aware of some disquiet that the script used for the simultaneous translation of *Shylock* was in Russian not Ukrainian, but the reality is that everyone at the performance would understand Russian whilst not everyone present could follow a performance in Ukrainian. The diplomatic excuse was that the Russian translation of *The Merchant of Venice* was superior to the local version and would best serve my play.

Some of the People, Some of the Time

I am a Jew. Hath not a Jew eyes? Hath not a Jew
hands, organs, dimensions, senses, affections,
passions, fed with the same food, hurt with the
same weapons, subject to the same diseases, healed
by the same means, warmed and cooled by the same
winter and summer as a Christian is? If you prick
us, do we not bleed? If you tickle us, do we not
laugh? If you poison us, do we not die . . . ?

Those are the most often quoted of Shylock's lines from
The Merchant of Venice. People who refuse to acknowledge
that Shakespeare might have been an anti-Semite cite
them as proof positive of his tolerance and humanity. Like
so many lines and speeches from Shakespeare, it is often
anthologised, taken out of context, and used to illustrate
or prove a point of view. But its context is all important,
and those lines form barely half of the whole of Shylock's
speech. He goes on:

. . . and if you wrong us, shall we not revenge?
If we are like you in the rest, we will resemble you
in that. If a Jew wrong a Christian, what is his
humility? Revenge! If a Christian wrong a Jew, what
should his sufferance be by Christian example?
Why, revenge! The villainy you teach me I will
execute, and it shall go hard but I will better the
instruction.

It is a speech as much justifying Shylock's intention to cut out Antonio's heart as it is a plea for equality. What makes it remarkable is that there is nothing else in the play to match its simple and direct appeal to a common humanity. Just as remarkable is that the lines are written in prose not verse, the form usually favoured by Shakespeare for expressing nobler sentiments.

Not everyone agrees that the speech puts its author on the moral high ground either. I had a discussion with Arnold Wesker about it: 'What's so admirable about admitting that a Jew has flesh and blood, appetites and vulnerabilities, just like a Christian?' he said. 'You could say almost the same things about a monkey! Where's the spiritual dimension, the acknowledgement that Shylock has a soul and a right to his beliefs and practices?'

In my show, I subvert the speech somewhat by playing it as it might have been seen by Shakespeare's audience. The second act begins with a blackout whilst I find myself centre stage. A bright white spotlight snaps on and reveals me wearing a grotesque false nose and a bright ginger curly wig, the very emblems which would have identified Shylock, and, indeed, Tubal, as a Jew to the playgoers at the Globe. Just in case my audience might not get the message, I stick my tongue out obscenely once or twice before launching into a high-pitched and rather hysterical rendition of 'I am a Jew . . . !' I get a few nervous laughs at my pantomimic display, but just before I speak the word 'revenge', I whip off the nose and wig and assume my natural voice register to finish the speech as *my* Shylock. I have to admit that it is rather a coup. I also have to admit that it was Frank Barrie's idea.

Occasionally, a rabbi or a high-school teacher in the States will take me to task for not delivering the speech

properly. By 'properly', I think they mean slowly and sentim-
entally, but I will not acquiesce. Only once have I decided
not to do the speech as rehearsed and that was a decision
made halfway through a performance. And it was in the
United Arab Emirates.

I very rarely turn down a booking, but I did have some
reservations about doing a demonstrably pro-Jewish play
in the heart of Arabia, and at a very sensitive time. The
jovial Brit who ran the venue seemed very sanguine about it
when I asked if there had been any objections to my visit.

'None at all, old boy. Mind you, we haven't put the word
Shylock on the posters. They just say: "Gareth Armstrong
presents scenes from William Shakespeare's *The Merchant
of Venice*." So long as we said the word "Shakespeare" the
censor didn't even ask to see a script!'

It turned out to be a dinner-theatre event where I came
on between the main course and the pudding. It was a
mixed audience of locals, smartly dressed in crisp white
jellabas and headdresses, and ex-pats in dinner jackets and
long frocks. It was fairly obvious from the beginning that
most of the audience, maybe even some of the Muslims,
had enthusiastically enjoyed the wines that accompanied
their pricey dinner. The show started ominously with
everyone laughing at almost every line, even the ones that
aren't meant to be funny. This is never a good sign because
eventually that sort of audience tires itself out and after
half an hour or so fall silent as the grave, or just into a deep
sleep. Sure enough, the merriment was soon over, but it
was replaced by a kind of laughter I had not expected to
hear. A sizeable section of the audience were not going to
give in to my sympathetic view of Shylock as a man more
sinned against than sinning. Their laughter now came only
occasionally and nearly always at Shylock and his plight. I
began to be embarrassed at my adopted middle-European

accent, my homburg, my shrugs and smatterings of Yiddish. It felt as if I was not confounding but colluding in their stereotypical image of Shakespeare's Jew.

The stage had been assembled at one end of a ballroom and my dressing room was a few square feet curtained off at the side. The only lavatory accessible to me was the same one that the audience used. Thinking that they would all have returned to their seats after what had seemed an interminable interval, I dashed out of a side door for an urgent pee. There was just one white portly man swaying slightly at a urinal. He was not at all phased by taking a piss with Shylock.

'Jolly, jolly good!' he slurred. 'Shame the wife and I can't stay for the next bit . . . early start in the morning. Just tell me . . . Shakespeare not really my thing . . . does the old yid get his comeuppance?'

I could hear that the entr'acte music for the second half had just started, so I excused myself and left him there. I suppose I could honestly have answered that, yes, indeed, Shylock does get his comeuppance, but how unsatisfactory it would have been to satisfy him. I did not bother to put on the wig and nose, and I did the opening speech just like the rabbi would have liked to hear it. I have no idea whether it reversed any prejudices, but at least nobody laughed.

A self-righteous glow isn't the inevitable reward for try-ing to manipulate your audience. An earnest young Greek woman arrived unannounced backstage just after a performance in Athens, and framed herself in the door-way of my dressing room. 'How is your play so . . . so . . . ?' She paused, conjuring with both her expressive hands the exact word. I would have liked to help her: poignant, stir-ring, heartfelt? ' . . . so biased?' she rasped at length.

There followed a three-minute tirade about the parti-ality of my historical perspective. Why hadn't I mentioned the six-day war, the Intifada, the tyranny of the Zionists? I found myself almost apologising for not having written the play she had wanted to see. Feebly, I insisted that my sympathy for Shylock inevitably extended to the suffering of his people. 'It's not a question of sympathy,' she said implacably. 'Your play is politically dishonest. What you present is just pro-Jewish propaganda.' She left. I don't know what surprised me most; her verdict, her vehemence or the enduring power of live theatre to arouse such passion.

All the same, I felt relieved that for the next performance of *Shylock*, I would be sitting anonymously in the audience, and seeing what the Italians would make of Eugenio Allegri's performance.

Back to the Ghetto

Eugenio Allegri is one of north Italy's most popular comic actors, his previous one-man show based on Cyrano de Bergerac had been a triumph. Also the movie of *Life is Beautiful*, in which he features, won an Oscar for Best Foreign Film. His debut as *Shylock* was at a gala performance to an exclusively invited audience of the artistic and academic glitterati of Venice. Expectations were high.

What the audience didn't know was that Eugenio was not limbering up for his performance, but miles away, lying prone on a hospital bed in Turin, nursing and cursing an injured knee. In his place, they were going to get an actor, unknown to them, playing in a foreign language. I was beginning to regret my heroic intervention. Then, one by one, those beautiful young women, whom I had sent off to collect my miscellany of props and costumes, all arrived back, proudly bearing each and every one of them, including the box of Imodium. I wonder what is the Italian for *fait accompli*?

How Eugenio hurt his knee I am not quite sure, but I think he blames the stage set devised for *Shylock* by a very enthusiastic design team. In contrast to my rather arbitrary scattering of furniture, and Manel's minimalist look in the Spanish production, the stage is dominated by tall dark panels, painted to look like the damp brick walls of Venice and disfigured with the crude graffiti that even that serene city is plagued with. On the floor is a pattern of raised wooden platforms, the very platforms used by the city authorities to keep feet dry when Venice floods. It's a lovely image, and a very versatile setting. By all accounts, Eugenio leapt between the platforms, lay prone across them, sat and dangled his feet from them into the imaginary waters and generally made the most of them in his very animated interpretation of the play.

When I got onto that stage to take his place, with only a few hours before the curtain was due to go up, I chickened out of using the platforms at all. The way my knees were feeling I would have buckled at the first jump and had to go into traction alongside Eugenio. Instead, the platforms were arranged in a purely decorative way upstage, while I worked in the empty space below them.

Luca improvised a simple lighting plot from the elaborate rig arranged for Eugenio and brought out some of his huge CD collection of opera to find some suitable music for use before the show and in the interval. We even found time for a frenetic couple of hours' rehearsal.

As the house started to fill, the audience's expectant chattering made me almost catatonic with nerves. I contemplated diving out of my dressing-room window into the adjacent canal. All that stopped me was the thought of that obituary in *The Stage*: 'A body recovered from the Grand Canal has been identified as Gareth Armstrong, an actor best known for his work on *The Archers*, radio's longest-running soap opera . . .'

Silence. The music had stopped. I jammed on my homburg and dashed up to the wings. Luca, transformed by his velvet dinner jacket from frantic director to cool impresario, was addressing the audience. I understood barely a word of what he was saying but there was no mistaking those sighs which followed the juxtaposition of Eugenio's name and mine. I thought back to poor Lewis Jones waiting to go on for Laurence Olivier as the Jew. There was polite applause at the end of Luca's speech, but I distinctly heard the tipping-up of half-a-dozen seats before the lights slowly faded and Shylock entered to face his fellow citizens.

Acknowledgements

Thanks, thanks . . .

Many of the individuals whose co-operation and generosity I most value have not featured in this book. Below are people, some known and some unknown to me, who have influenced and assisted the journeys that I have chronicled.

My main theme has been the genesis and progress of a play I wrote in 1997 and which I am still performing. In the intervening years, the play and I have gone through many transformations, but both owe a huge debt to the personnel who first got us up and running. Jonathan Church and Rebecca Morland, respectively Artistic and Executive Directors of the Salisbury Playhouse at the time, offered the encouragement and then the means to launch the project. Their production staff, Chris Bagust, Peter Hunter, Gina Hills, Brum Gardner and Ian Burrage, mounted the show and it was ingeniously costumed by Henrietta Worrall-Thomson and her wardrobe team from a non-existent budget. The fact that all the original props and costumes are still in use is less a testimony to the care I take of them than the skill of their construction.

The original music was composed by Simon Slater and it was the first of my many collaborations with this brilliant musician. Whilst recognising that incidental music is just that, Simon brings an originality and flexibility to his work that is rapidly gaining him recognition, and probably means I won't be able to afford him next time.

From Salisbury, via the Edinburgh Festival, I got reacquainted with the British Council and all its works.

Most people in Britain have little idea what the British Council is. Overseas however, when it makes its presence felt, the organisation does wonderful work in promoting educational and cultural co-operation. I am truly grateful to them and the London-based personnel in the Performing Arts Department for fuelling the magic carpet which has taken me so rewardingly around the world.

At the time of writing, my most recent performance of *Shylock,* at the Lincoln Center in New York, was not the same show which started its life in Salisbury. It's shorter for a start, and it's lightened up a bit. In the years between, the play and my playing have inevitably changed. Disparate spaces, audiences, and locations dictate that the play is organic, and though the next performance may not be better than the last it will certainly be different. I genuinely don't get bored with performing the same piece over and over again. What I do get, occasionally, is lonely. When I am not fortunate enough to be touring with a friend, doubling as my technician or manager, I rely on the readiness of my hosts to befriend me and, almost without exception, they live up to and exceed my expectations. From Kandy in Sri Lanka to Kiel in Northern Germany, and from Monclova in Mexico to Mumbai in India I have been on the receiving end of the most exceptional warmth and hospitality. In America and Canada this is especially true of the Jewish communities who embrace me as one of their own, and will use any holiday feast from Thanksgiving to Purim as an excuse to welcome me into their homes.

I would never have got to the States with *Shylock* were it not for an initial invitation from Alan Dessen, a Shakespeare professor at the University of Chapel Hill, North Carolina. Unlike many academics, Alan respects and appreciates the actor's contribution to Shakespearean scholarship, and is an invaluable ally. Whatever new project

I confront him with, his responses are always thoughtful and thorough, and he and his wife Cynthia transmit powerful transatlantic waves of encouragement.

Encouragement or assistance, patience or perseverance, wisdom or generosity have each, and sometimes all, been offered to me by the following friends and colleagues not mentioned at greater length. Those I have left out, I know will add the gift of indulgence to their virtues: Sushma K. Bahl, Mary Barrie, Theresa Barton, Valentine Boinitsky, Debs Callan, Peter Campbell, Susan Chapman, Andrew Christon, Ronnie Church, Andrew Connolly, Eunice Crook, Codruta Cruceanu, Michael Curry, Brian Daniels, Ariel Friedman, Suzan Friedman, John Griffiths, Chandrika Grover, Emma Hands, Judi Herman, Richard Jordan, Haris Karnezi, Alexander Kirilenko, Rachel Kruger, Patrick Lau, Rob Leetham, Hugh Levinson, Christopher Luscombe, John Macfarlane, Jyoti Makihja, Mark Makin, Miriam Margolyes, Susana Martinez-Ostos, Jane Maud, Malcolm McKee, Nicolette McKenzie, Chrysula Melidou, Frank Middlemass, Ranmali Mirchandani, Janet Patch, Roopa Patel, Ecaterina Petreanu, Martin Platt, David Roper, Toni Rumbau, Jan Ryan, Mallika Sarabhai, Mrinalini Sarabhai, Henry Schvey, Alexander Shpilyuk, Patrick Spottiswoode, Maya Sundararajan, Geoffrey Toone, Sally Vaughan, Peter Wilcocks; Alun and Gwen Armstrong, Edmund and Megan Marsden, Anne and Jim McMeehan Roberts, Danny and Maureen Nissim, Paul and Viveka Smith, Hugh and Natasha Templeton, Bronwen and Rhodri Thomas, Jean and Peter Wilmot Dear, James Wellman and David Swift.

*

. . . and ever thanks

I am a slow reader, so it's a mixed blessing that there is more written about Shylock than any other Shakespearean character apart from Hamlet. I think I've waded through most of it. But since a bibliography might suggest that this book was the result of earnest researches, I just draw attention to some of those writers who illuminate the impact Shylock makes on the stage as well as in the classroom. Harley Granville Barker's *Preface to The Merchant of Venice* has all the usual theatrical common sense he brings to each of those invaluable essays. His is one of the dozen useful contributions that make up Harold Bloom's compendium volume: *Major Literary Characters: Shylock*, where Mr Bloom, of course, makes his own robust presence felt, as he also does in *Shakespeare – The Invention of the Human*. John Barton's *Playing Shakespeare* explores the two memorable performances by Patrick Stewart and David Suchet for the Royal Shakespeare Company. Toby Lelyveld's *Shylock on the Stage* gives riveting accounts of the great historical performances from Macklin to Irving, as well as two chapters irresistibly called 'Lesser Lights' and 'Shylock Distorted'. It stops some years short of chronicling Laurence Olivier's performance, and although I must have read everything written about his Shylock, most accounts are quite inadequate as I can testify, having witnessed it for myself. *Shylock and Shakespeare* by Abraham Morevski is a quirky but heartfelt contribution, as is Diana Valk's biographical memoir of her husband Frederick, *Shylock for a Summer*.

John Gross's *Shylock – Four Hundred Years in the Life of a Legend* was certainly the most influential single volume I devoured, and James Shapiro's *Shakespeare and the Jews* is full of fascinating, and often shocking revelations.

Nick Hern not only publishes a highly influential list of theatre books, but even manages to find time to edit some of them. When he returned the first draft of this volume to me, covered in comments and corrections, I had a distinct feeling of déjà vu. The handwriting was worse than I remembered but the wry, sometimes acerbic, always helpful notes were not so different from the ones which filled the margins of my student essays on *Sturm und Drang* or the Theatre of the Absurd. Nick, though only marginally my senior, was one of my lecturers in the Drama Department of Hull University in the late 1960s. His humour, patience and perceptiveness are intact, and he has now wisely surrounded himself with staff who possess not only those qualities but that additional and most enviable attribute – youthful enthusiasm. My thanks to Tamara von Werthern, Jemima Rhys-Evans, Robin Booth and especially to Matt Applewhite.

My only reservation about writing these acknowledgements at the end rather than at the beginning of this book was that the great and gracious recipient of my last word of thanks would be relegated to the bottom line of the final page. But as her name on the front cover may be the reason why you picked up this book in the first place, maybe she should be the last word. My thanks to Judi Dench.